THE OAKWOOD LIBRARY OF RAILWAY HISTORY NUMBER 66

THE CATERHAM RAILWAY

The Story of a Feud – and its Aftermath

by
Jeoffry Spence

THE OAKWOOD PRESS

DEDICATED

to

THE PROMOTERS OF THE CATERHAM RAILWAY COMPANY

without whose courage there would have been no town of Caterham

and to

THE DIRECTORS OF THE SOUTH-EASTERN AND THE LONDON, BRIGHTON & SOUTH COAST RAILWAY COMPANIES

whose acrimonious contentions and internecine warfare have helped to enliven this narrative, and who spared no efforts to bring the history of their unfortunate victim to a premature conclusion.

ISBN 0 85361 325 7

First edition 1952
This revised edition 1986

Printed and Bound by Bocardo Press, Cowley, Oxford

BY THE SAME AUTHOR

Victorian and Edwardian Railways
Victorian and Edwardian Railway Travel
Surviving Steam Railways (*with Anthony Lambert*)
The British Railway Station (*with Gordon Biddle*)
Closed Passenger Lines of Great Britain 1827–1947 (*with M.D. Greville*)

Cover photograph The 3-coach empty stock being propelled out of Caterham station by DS377 No. 35 *Morden* on a wet 5 August 1956. *R.C. Riley*

All photographs from the author's collection unless otherwise stated.

Published by
The OAKWOOD PRESS
P.O. Box 122, Headington, Oxford

Contents

Appendices

Acknowledgements

The Bibliography in connexion with this book is so vast that it is impossible to quote everything into which research has been made; it includes almost every contemporary railway journal, and other publications from *The Gentleman's Magazine* to *Debrett's Peerage*.

The author is very much indebted to many people who have assisted in the work: the late Mr H.A. Vallance for help in checking much of the information; to Mr R.C. Riley for valuable assistance with the locomotive notes; to Mr C.F. Wells for information regarding rolling-stock and headcodes; to Mr R.P. Angus Lewis for his excellent maps and diagrams; to Mr C. Hamilton Ellis for his delightful line drawing, and for certain advice; to Mr Rushworth, of Kingston County Hall, who remained placid and tolerant when asked for the original plans of all railways projected in the Caterham district; to Miss Betty Thirsk for frequent advice on how to write English correctly, and for typing out so much original copy (usually to find that it had immediately to be changed owing to fresh information coming in); to the British Transport Commission for permission to study the Minutes of the South-Eastern and Brighton Railways; and to innumerable officials at Waterloo and elsewhere on the Southern, who have patiently answered questions for so long that they now regard me, willy-nilly, as part of the office equipment – with special mention of Mr J. Young, of the Chief Civil Engineers Department, who showed great interest and spent a good deal of his spare time hunting for information to help me.

J.G.S.

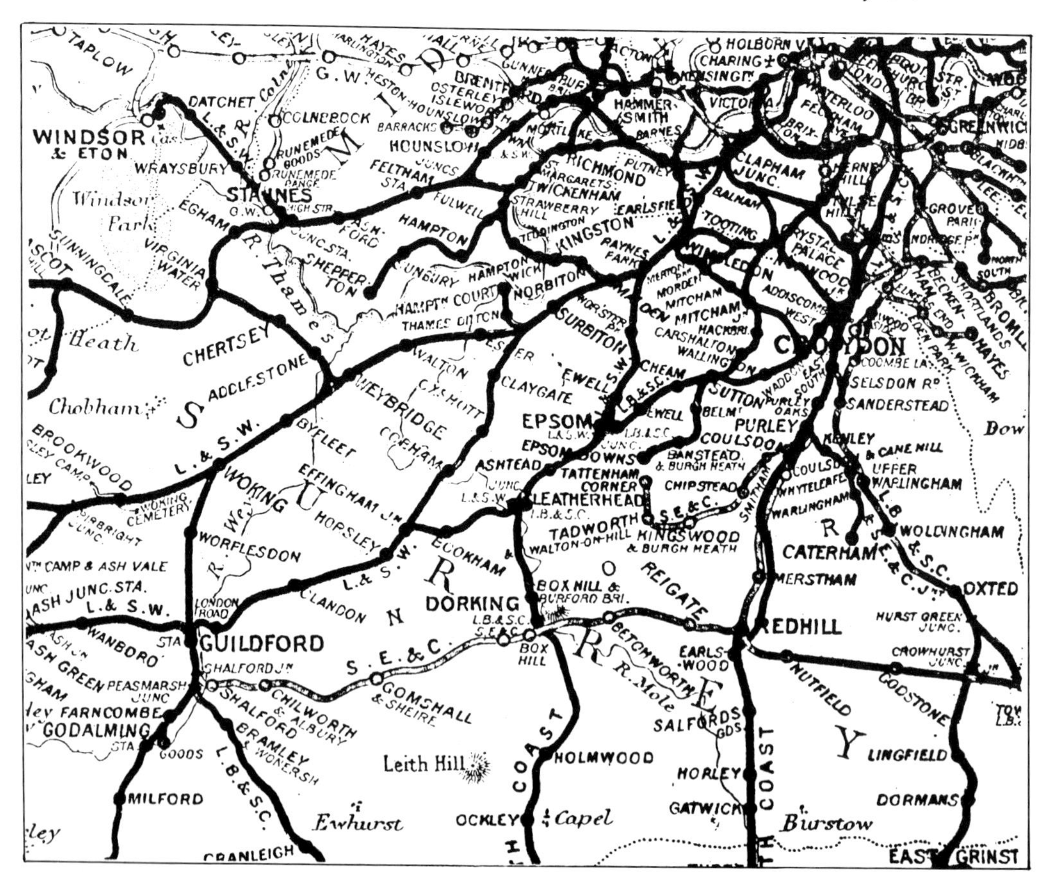

The RCH map of 1920 showing the Caterham branch and surrounding railways.

Introduction to 1986 Edition

Since the publication of this book in 1952, not a great deal has happened to make travel on the Caterham line as much of a tourist attraction as it was in the middle of the 19th century. Indeed, from the point of view of commuters, if one takes into consideration the difference in population and the necessity of travel, they probably did as well then. Admittedly the journey time was four minutes longer!

To look on the bright side, there are now through trains between London and Caterham in off-peak hours, instead of that hellish wait at Purley. Unfortunately, we are all nowadays aware of the much-used 'in' word 'retrenchment', which means: 'If it doesn't pay, cut it out'. Just for once we should not blame the Government, or British Railways but the passenger (I refuse to use their idiotic 'in' expression 'British Rail'). The passenger is expected to patronise his line and not go rushing off in cars to a distant station several miles away, where a train will get him to London two minutes earlier; that sort of thing is for emergencies. If only we could learn to relax, travelling would be so much simpler. Personally, I always like to catch the train before the one I really need to (exceptions being places like Inverness) and don't rely on bus connexions, which usually run to a timetable on paper only.

However, we had a wonderful Centenary celebration in 1956, that no one who was there will forget, and this book is still intended as a history of the Caterham Railway and the surrounding district, and I should not really let myself be drawn into the sordid area of politics; railway or otherwise. If I did, I might not live to start preparing for the bi-centenary in the year 2056. I wonder how 'improved' this district will look by then?

The 1952 edition has been left virtually intact, except for correction of the odd error and addition. Only towards the end has there been much re-writing, in view of the fact that what was virtually contemporary matter at the time is now thirty-year-old history.

My thanks are still due to those who were acknowledged in the 1952 edition; due again, too, to Frank Wells for re-checking facts in the now changed circumstances; and to Ronald Dabbs and Brian Dagwell for help with photographs; and to the Bourne Society for the local history. This Society came into existence shortly before the Caterham centenary, and is now the largest local history society in the country.

Lastly, my thanks to The Oakwood Press for a new enlarged edition containing more plans and illustrations. I have always been grateful for the fact that copies of the 1952 edition never seem to appear in second-hand bookshops and I can only hope it means owners of copies found them too valuable to part with!

January 1986 J.G.S.

A busy scene in the high street of Caterham Valley in 1926.

A fine period photograph of Caterham station, taken before 1870, showing locomotive and train just arriving. The goods shed, on left, was then an engine shed. The cottages on the skyline (*top right*) were part of 'Paddy's Heaven', built for the men who constructed the line.

Introduction

Writing the history of the Caterham Railway did not prove so easy a task as I had at one time imagined it would be. Many of the facts which have come to light were discovered only after prolonged research, and continual importuning of the various officials at Waterloo Station, who were an example of patience and courtesy which it is not always easy to find in these rather hectic days. In spite of every effort, the story is in some respects incomplete, for many details and anecdotes, especially of its early days, have been lost in the mists of the past. I must apologise, too, to those readers who are interested only in locomotives. The information about Caterham locomotives in the independent days is very scanty, and under the South-Eastern it received, like most branch lines, only the part-worn engines from the rest of the system, which often finished their last days there.

I have at times been rude and scathing about the attitude adopted by the South-Eastern Railway, but I have never, in my heart, felt malicious about it. For some reason – and I am sure it would baffle any psycho-analyst – the South-Eastern captured my imagination in my very early days, and I have remained loyal to it ever since. Even the conceit of the London & North-Western Railway in considering itself the Premier Line (and I am not prepared to argue with its admirers), or the rather ponderous and dignified efficiency of the Great Western, did not deflect me from my course.

Only after 1899, when the South-Eastern joined forces with the London, Chatham & Dover, does my interest falter a little, for I always had faint, and I am sure unjust, suspicions that the 'Chatham' was a more tiresome, if not less efficient, affair.

With the London, Chatham & Dover pricking away on the one side, the South-Eastern yet had time to wage war against the Brighton, a feud that had been in operation since their opening days. Into this whirlpool of strife the Caterham Railway[1] fell.

Some may be misled into thinking this is an attack on British Railways for not making more improvements on the line, but they will be disappointed. I have dealt with passengers' complaints as fairly as possible, but I have no sympathy with the inveterate grumbler who thinks he is the only pebble on the beach. Generally, that type has no idea how a railway functions, nor of the difficulties in producing the magnificent service to the public that the Southern Railway built up under the guidance of that most capable and respected of Chief General Managers, the late Sir Herbert Walker.

There is a considerable amount of detail in this history that, on the face of it, does not appear in the least necessary. Who cares whether Kenley was at one time reduced to the uninspiring level of a mere

[1]This was one of the subjects of the *Relations between the Brighton and South-Eastern Companies*, in an obscure little book discovered at Waterloo.

halt? Or that the first slip-coach introduced at Caterham Junction was in January 1861? The railway historian, however, very often does care about meticulous detail of events and dates, and these should, if known, be included.

Some may wonder at my idea of trying to unravel the history of what is now little more than a rather dull suburban backwater. This book has been written for several reasons. Firstly, because it is my line and I wanted to write about it, and because I believe that any historical knowledge should be handed on for the sake of the students of the future; for research work, though of absorbing interest, can be very frustrating without some foundation upon which one can build. Secondly, because a large body of men are interested in railway history. Thirdly, because local people are often glad to know that 'their line' had a more colourful past than one might, perhaps, think; and lastly, because I have an opinion which I have the honour to share with some of the great men of this country, that history of any sort, far from being a nostalgic outlet for the emotionally unstable, or a study for intellectual snobs, is of real importance in teaching us about those mistakes which can help to guide us on to the right path for the future.

A fine view of a train on the Caterham Branch seen here between Kenley and Whyteleafe on 21 July 1901. *P.J. Mallett Collection*
Courtesy National Railway Museum

Chapter One

The Caterham of the Past

The modern town of Caterham, lying as it does among the high ridges and valleys of the North Downs, barely twenty miles from London, owes its development to the opening of the railway in 1856. These valleys, described by John Aubrey, the traveller and naturalist, in the seventeenth century, as 'stored with wild thyme, sweet marjoram, barnell [darnel], boscage and beeches,' though nowadays marred by the builder's hand in some places, still contain the soft beauty so envied by those who live in the cramped areas of the less fortunate suburbs.

Here, too, in the main Caterham valley, at one time known as Stoneham Bottom, is the same Bourne which alarmed the inhabitants of the district in past centuries by appearing at intervals and flooding the valley down to Smitham Bottom – always conveniently before some remarkable event or catastrophe, which earned it the title of Woe Water. Today the Bourne has been subjugated, and driven into underground culverts and drains, where it can do little harm.

There are in reality two towns of Caterham: Caterham Valley, with its shopping centre, railway station and main public buildings – a portion of the parish which before the railway days consisted of perhaps half a dozen buildings, scattered here and there; and Caterham-on-the-Hill, the old village, now somewhat desecrated by the Barracks, the Asylum, and a great deal of ugly building in the irregular fashion of the later Victorian era.

As a place, Caterham has not the historical associations of its larger and more important neighbours, such as Reigate and Croydon. The original village was never on any main highway, but remained through the centuries a small, isolated, but rather snug hamlet, with its church, its inn, and its two manor houses. These two manors, without any adjunct to either to distinguish one from the other, were both known by the name of Caterham only, until the appearance of the names Salmons and Portley.

Caterham is not mentioned by name in Domesday Book, but there was, in fact, an unnamed Manor, which is believed to be Caterham, held by one Azor, in the reign of Edward the Confessor. After the Norman Conquest, this manor was assigned to Robert de Wateville, and held by him for Richard de Tunbridge, one of William the Conqueror's Anglo-Norman barons. Domesday adds that there was 'wood which yields pannage for five swine,' and that there was a church, which supports the supposition that the present Church of St Lawrence (*c.* 1095) had a predecessor. In all probability the original manor was close to the church. Unfortunately, almost exactly the same description fits the nearby parish of Chelsham, also held by Robert de Watevile, so really this has yet to be proved.

The actual origin of the name Caterham would appear to be from the Celtic *cader* – a hill-fort, possibly with reference to the old Iron Age camp at Whitehill. It should perhaps be noted that compounds of the Anglo-Saxon word *ham* with a pre-English word like *cader* are very rare. The earliest form of the name that has been found is twelfth century, and, except for variations in spelling, and the fact that it was pronounced 'Catterham' until about a century ago, it has remained the same. It is interesting to note that in the nearby parish of Oxted is Caterfield Bridge, known as Cateringforde in the fourteenth century, which is considered by reliable authority to represent a name-formation of a much earlier date, but which would have meant 'ford of the people from Caterham,' a name that would have arisen at a time when Caterham could be regarded as forming a unit of population.[1]

Through the Caterham valley runs the old Roman road from Portslade to London, traces of which have been found along the eastern side of the valley. Crossed by this on the summit of the main ridge of the North Downs is the so-called 'Pilgrims' Way' from Winchester to Canterbury. Whether this track was ever used by pilgrims is now considered a matter of doubt; that any did use it is purely incidental. For all that, it is an ancient trackway of interest to the historian, passing through some of the loveliest scenery in Surrey.

And so through the centuries this little village remained in its wooded downland retreat, almost oblivious to the outer world. Down the Lewes road, through Croydon and over Riddles Down – for the main road then took this hilly route – came the stage-coaches; by the *Rose and Crown* at the foot of Riddles Down, the *Half Moon*[2] in Stoneham Bottom, to the *White Hart*[3] at Godstone, and onwards to East Grinstead.

During the early part of the nineteenth century, coaches made daily trips to and from London, East Grinstead and the South, passing along the Caterham valley. Pigot's Directory for 1839 records three coaches daily, and one extra three days a week, between London and the South, calling at Godstone.

In 1801 came the first railway in the world to receive an Act of Parliament – the Surrey Iron Railway from the Thames at Wandsworth to Croydon[4] with a branch to Carshalton. The main line was opened on 26 July 1803.[5]

[1]English Place Names Society: Surrey.

[2]Situated a short distance south of the present roundabout at Wapses Lodge.

[3]For a period was known as the *Clayton Arms*.

[4]Bill received Royal Assent 21 May 1801 (41 Geo. III, cap. 33).

[5]For a full and instructive account of both the Surrey Iron, and Croydon, Merstham & Godstone Railways, see *Early Railways in Surrey* by Charles E. Lee, and *Grand Surrey Iron Railway* by F.G. Bing.

At this time the English Channel and Straits of Dover were dangerous for shipping, owing to the Napoleonic Wars, and schemes were considered for connecting London with the south coast at Portsmouth, to obviate the necessity of bringing ships right round to the Thames. The Surrey Iron Railway was a start in providing this overland communication, and this was followed by a separate undertaking, the Croydon, Merstham & Godstone Iron Railway, for which powers were obtained on 17 May 1803. In this Act[1] it is described as 'a Railway from or from near a Place called Pitlake Meadow, in the Town of Croydon, to or near to the Town of Reigate, in the County of Surrey, with a collateral Branch from the said Railway, at or near a Place called Merstham, in the Parish of Merstham, to or near to a Place called Godstone Green, in the Parish of Godstone, all in the said County of Surrey.' Among those employed in the construction of this line was one Edward Banks, a man of great original talent as a builder and engineer, who was later associated with Waterloo, Southwark and London Bridges.[2]

Despite a certain doubt about the opening date of this line, Mr Lee, whose authority on these matters need not be questioned, thinks that 24 July 1805 is correct. It ran from Croydon over the Banstead Downs by Purley, to the Greystone Lime Works at Merstham. The extension to Godstone was never built, though traces of earthworks beyond Merstham indicate that some attempt was made to carry it further. Neither was the intended remainder of the main line to Reigate – with its ultimate destination Portsmouth – ever constructed. In October 1805 came the victory at Trafalgar, which reduced the urgent necessity of overland communication to the south coast, with the result that both lines were of value only for local needs – the cheaper conveyance of coal, lime, and agricultural produce. As far as is known, no passengers ever were carried officially. As will be seen, the construction of the London & Brighton Railway sealed the fate of the Croydon, Merstham & Godstone Line, and the Surrey Iron Railway was closed a few years later on 31 August 1846.

Remains of the Croydon, Merstham & Godstone are to be seen in several places, especially in the Merstham district, where are to be found lengths of cuttings and sets of bridge parapets (now sadly in need of repair). Cottages near the terminus at Merstham, said to have been the stables for the horses that drew the trains, and permanent way with stone sleepers, now lie under the M23 motorway. A length of original rails and sleepers, set up for preservation by the *Joliffe Arms*, near Merstham, disappeared some years ago, presumed stolen for scrap.

[1] 43 Geo. III, cap. 35.
[2] Measom's *Guide to the L.B. & S.C.R.*, 1853, p. 21. Banks was buried at Chipstead.

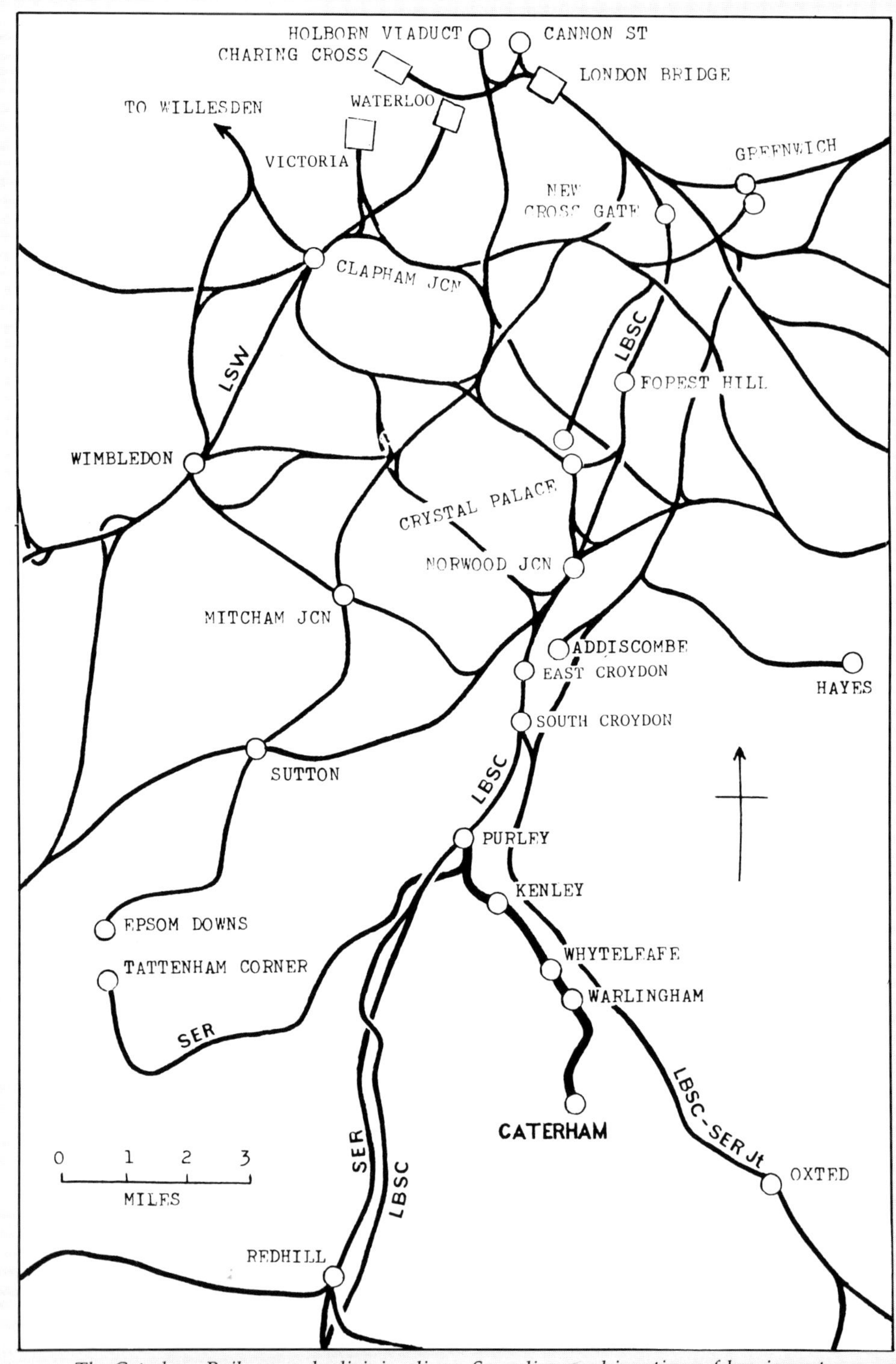

The Caterham Railway and adjoining lines. Some lines and junctions of less importance are not included.

Chapter Two

The Opening of the Brighton and South-Eastern Main Lines

There were many schemes for connecting London with the fashionable resort of Brighton, but only one of them calls for notice here. This is the present line, incorporated by an Act of 15 July 1837[1] under the title of London & Brighton Railway. In order to put it in its true perspective, however, we must turn to one of its constituent parts, the London & Croydon Railway, authorised by an Act of 12 June 1835. This line built its Croydon terminus at the present West Croydon station, on the site of the basin of the Croydon Canal which it had purchased for £40,259, and closed in August 1836. This railway, in its turn, did not reach London over its own metals, but ran over the London & Greenwich Railway (opened 1836) from Corbetts Lane, north of New Cross, to London Bridge.

The London & Croydon Railway was opened 5 June 1839, with stations at New Cross, Dartmouth Arms,[2] Sydenham, Penge[3], Anerley,[4] and Jolly Sailor.[5]

The London & Brighton joined the London & Croydon 'on Penge Common' (i.e. south of the Jolly Sailor station) and was opened to Hayward's Heath on 12 July 1841, and to Brighton the September following. The line was planned to run over part of the Croydon, Merstham & Godstone Railway, which would have caused so much damage to the latter line that the London & Brighton was compelled, by Section 40 of its Act, to buy the whole of it. Purchase was completed, and the Company's effects sold by September 1838.

In the meantime, the South-Eastern Railway, which had been incorporated in 1836, was authorised to leave the London & Croydon Railway at its Croydon terminus, and follow a route which would have paralleled the Brighton line as far as Purley. At this point the South-Eastern was to turn off, up the Caterham valley as far as Wapses Lodge, where it was to follow a more south-easterly course through the hills to Oxted, and on to Edenbridge and Tonbridge.

On the incorporation of the Brighton Railway the following year it was realised by Parliament that this paralleling would be a financial disadvantage, and as more than one exit to the south from London had been refused, the South-Eastern Company's Act was amended to authorise a junction with the Brighton at Redhill.[6] To all intents and

---

[1] 1 Vic., cap. 119.

[2] Renamed Forest Hill 1846.

[3] Closed about 1840 and reopened as Penge Bridges 1 July 1863.

[4] William Sanderson, a Scot, built a house here and called it 'Anerly' from the Scots word 'lonely'; he offered the Croydon Railway part of his property free of charge on condition they built a station there and called it 'Anerly' (Hodgson: *Notes on the History of Penge*).

[5] Renamed Norwood 1846. The original Jolly Sailor station house was to be seen on the up side, about 100 yards north of the present station (opened 1 June 1859) until a decade or so ago.

[6] This followed an amendment of 1837 for a line from near Merstham to Edenbridge *via* Godstone Green.

purposes, therefore, the South-Eastern would have had to travel over the London & Greenwich, London & Croydon and London & Brighton Railways before reaching its own metals. The Brighton and South-Eastern were authorised to construct the line from Croydon to Redhill jointly, each taking, and paying for, a half of it. In actual fact, the Brighton constructed the line, and handed over to the South-Eastern for £300,000 the southern half, from Stoat's Nest to Redhill, when that Company opened its main line to Tonbridge on 26 May 1842.

During the construction of this section of the line, trouble was reported from the Merstham Tunnel area, where the contractor was having difficulty with the men engaged in the great cuttings. They complained bitterly that no beer could be got in the locality, and at one time a general strike was threatened. It was reported[1] that the nearest place where beer could be bought was at a little shop kept by an old woman at Woodmansterne,[2] boys being employed to fetch it at a half-penny a journey.

Work on the Brighton Railway was pushed ahead rapidly, and on 28 June 1841, inspectors made an experimental excursion to Hayward's Heath, and 'the result was all that could be desired.'[3] In July, 300 extra men were taken on to complete the line to Brighton, in readiness for the opening which was fixed for Tuesday, 21 September. Two nights before this, *The Times* reports[4] that 'the inhabitants of Brighton were . . . thrown into considerable anxiety by a delay of upwards of an hour in the arrival of the last train, and the subsequent reports that one, two or three persons had been killed by a concussion on the line. On that evening, Mr Barratt, one of the inspectors of the works on the line, was despatched down the line delivering to the policemen at the different stations the new signal flags to be used at the opening on the Tuesday. The engine ran into a train of earth-waggons drawn by horses near Hooleylane and smashed the waggons to pieces, the engine being also thrown off the line by the concussion. There were no injuries.'

The original Brighton Railway stops between Croydon and Reigate were at Godstone Road, Stoat's Nest, and Merstham. Between Croydon and Merstham there was an almost complete lack of population and it is rather surprising to find any sort of station at all. Godstone Road, seven miles from the village, was merely a name, and can have attracted little traffic. On 30 September 1847 it was closed (despite a minute of the Brighton Directors at a meeting the previous April that 'a house be erected there for the Clerk, at a cost of

[1] *Railway Magazine*, Vol. XVI, p. 346.
[2] This may refer to the *Red Lion* at Stoat's Nest.
[3] *The Times*, 1 July 1841.
[4] *Ibid.*, 21 September 1841.

£127'). It remained in disuse until the opening of the Caterham Railway nine years later. Within a short time of the closing, a memorial was received from Mr Aglionby Aglionby, of Manor Cottage, Caterham,[1] complaining that he had been deprived of a train service.[2] The Brighton replied that, owing to the number of stations, Godstone Road had become an impediment to traffic.[3] The shelter on the platform was later moved to Bexhill.[4] Stoat's Nest, situated at a level-crossing where the Caterham–Coulsdon–Purley road now makes a double-bend under the main Brighton line, was optimistically intended for the use of passengers travelling to Epsom Race Course, eight miles away![5] This station, on the reopening of Godstone Road, became redundant, and was closed to passengers on 30 November 1856. The Stoat's Nest station of 1899 was some distance further south.[6]

Merstham station was originally half a mile south of the present one and was opened, it is understood, on 1 December 1841 in agreement with Lord Monson of Gatton Park. There was some sort of signal stop there from the opening, as it is shown, with Stoat's Nest and Godstone Road, in the pre-opening time-sheet of July 1841. It was closed, for no known reason, on 1 October 1843 and reopened 4 October 1844 after legal representations had been made by the family, the new station – opened the following year – not being ready. The old station (an excellent example of David Mocatta's architectural work for the smaller stations on the Brighton Railway) was severely damaged by enemy action in the last war and pulled down.

The nearby Merstham Tunnel, with its sinister reputation for murder and suicide was, in early days – perhaps only for a year or so – lighted by gas and whitewashed throughout. As the lamps were at eye-level, and on both sides of the tunnel, this must have been disturbing for passengers, especially those in open third-class carriages. It was intended also to be of service to drivers, who could see any obstruction ahead. The gas-works were some distance south of the present station, on the down side, where the Bletchingley and

[1]Usually, but erroneously, referred to as the 'Manor House'. Many years later it became Warlingham Golf Club House.

[2]Mr Aglionby always complained. *See p.* 23. Perhaps, as an MP, he had enough influence or hold over someone to have had Godstone Road opened in the first place.

[3]LB&SCR Minutes, 18 October 1847.

[4]LB&SCR Minutes, 3 January 1848.

[5]That the station was used by racegoers is evident from a report on Epsom Races (*Illustrated London News*, 28 May 1842): 'The activity that prevailed . . . at the Croydon Railway terminus, particularly since the "Stoat's Nest", to which that railway runs, is not more than six miles from Epsom . . . showed that the racing week had begun.'

[6]Stoat's Nest was the scene of a serious accident to a Brighton–London express on 29 January 1910, when the wheel of a carriage shifted on its axle, causing the greater part of the train to be derailed. The unusual name apparently filled the more nervous passenger with foreboding, and the station was re-christened 'Coulsdon & Smitham Downs', 1 June 1911. It was again re-named 'Coulsdon West' 9 July 1923 and finally settled down to 'Coulsdon North' 1 August 1923.

South Merstham roads join by the railway bridge. In 1845 the old gas pipes were used for signals to denote when a train had passed completely through the tunnel, by attaching an air chamber at each end, with an air pump. By this means, the air was exhausted, so that the policeman at one end could ring a bell, and blow a whistle at the other.[1]

Reigate station, shown on early time-sheets as 'Red-Hill and Reigate-Road' was by the old east to west road, nearly half a mile south of the present (Redhill) station, and was the source of one of the earlier conflicts between the Brighton and South-Eastern. The old station building was still to be seen opposite what was Earlswood Junction signal-box until the 1960s. On the opening of the Tonbridge line in 1842, the South-Eastern placed its 'Reigate' station on the Tonbridge side of the junction, with the result that Brighton passengers wishing to go into Kent had to turn out at the Brighton Company's station and make their own way down country lanes to the South-Eastern station. It would appear that Merstham was also used as a sort of interchange station for a short time. No doubt this would have been useful to the passenger accompanied by the inevitable cabin trunks, hatboxes and other impedimenta. On 19 March 1844 the Brighton acquired ground covering the present Redhill station, 'to be charged to the account of the South-Eastern Railway.'[2] It is to be presumed that this apparently sharp practice was known to the South-Eastern, who thereby became owners of the property and built the new Reigate station.[3] The Brighton closed its own station, and concentrated the traffic on the new South-Eastern station opened 16 April 1844.[4] A letter from the Brighton to the South-Eastern of that date requested that 'the station might be called "Reigate & Red Hill", and that the Finger Posts on the High Roads might have "To the Dover and Brighton Station" marked on them'.

By an Act of 27 July 1846 the London & Brighton and London & Croydon Railways were amalgamated under the title of the London, Brighton & South Coast Railway. The South-Eastern had already taken over the working of the London & Greenwich Railway on a 999-year lease in 1845. Thus the number of different companies between London Bridge and Redhill was reduced from four to two, of which the Brighton held the greater portion.

On 10 July 1848, the Brighton and South-Eastern Companies

[1]SER Minutes, 6 November 1845.

[2]Marked on the original London & Brighton Railway Deposit plans.

[3]Name altered to Reigate Junction on opening of Reading, Guildford & Reigate Railway to Dorking on 4 July 1849, and to Red Hill Junction in August 1858.

[4]It cannot have been a very substantial building as a SER report of 18 February 1858 remarks that 'a new station at Redhill is being erected owing to the decayed and rotten condition of the old structure.'

entered into an Agreement which included, *inter alia*, the following points:

1. The South-Eastern was to be permitted to run free of toll over the original London & Croydon line from Norwood to Corbetts Lane, and to stop at the intermediate stations for passenger purposes.
2. The Brighton was to be relieved of the £25,000 owing to the South-Eastern for the latter's work in widening the Greenwich lines between Corbetts Lane and London Bridge.
3. Both Companies undertook *not to make any new lines which penetrated each other's territory.*

No. 3 was the most important from the point of view of the future Caterham Railway, but fortunately for everybody's peace of mind at the time, it did not occur to anybody that this specific problem would ever arise at this point. As a definition of 'territory' they took the main London–Brighton and Redhill–Tonbridge railways as dividing lines. Anything north and east of these two was to become jealously guarded South-Eastern property.

Successor to the 'Q' Class was Wainwright's 'H' Class 0–4–4T. 1909 built No. 162 is seen at Caterham in 1913 with birdcage brake bogie stock. Driver Coe in charge. This engine was withdrawn in 1960. *Late Hemming Collection*

Francis Fuller, one time Chairman of the Caterham Railway Company.

The remains of Manor Cottage (damaged during World War II) seen here in 1952. This is where the 'first-class' dinner was held to celebrate the cutting of the first sod of the railway in 1855. The building has now been demolished.

Chapter Three

The Birth of the Caterham Railway

There is, unfortunately, no record as to who first mooted the idea of a railway to Caterham. The *Railway Record* wrote that Thomas Wright, the antiquarian, first suggested that the Caterham Valley should be opened up. The first Chairman was John Campbell Colquhoun of Chartwell, Westerham. The Directors were Charles Dingwall of Caterham, Alexander Beattie of Sydenham, who was a Director of the South-Eastern, Alfred Smith, farmer, of Tupwood, George Drew of Kenley House, who subscribed £3,000 towards the cost of construction, Alexander Greig, and Francis Fuller of Sydenham. Drew was later responsible for much of the building development in Caterham Valley, and built and lived at Beechanger Court, up the Harestone Valley. Fuller was also a character. He was born in Coulsdon, and had many business interests, being one of the promoters of the Great Exhibition of 1851. He saw the Derby run every year from 1821 to 1884 inclusive, which in itself seems something of a record.

Optimism must have run high at the time for, as mentioned earlier, Caterham was an insignificant place a hundred years ago. This 'off-the-map' village had, in 1851, a population of only 487[1] and lay on a hill a mile from the present terminus. The truth of the matter is that the railway was not so much intended to serve the people of Caterham as to convey the stone from the quarries and labyrinth of tunnels which run under the ridge about 1½ miles to the south. These quarries had been worked from ancient times, for beneath the chalk surface lay a thick layer of firestone which, although soft when quarried, and easily worked, became extremely hard after exposure to the air, and was particularly valuable for furnaces and chimneys. Local firestone was considered superior to any other, and used in furnaces as far off as Bristol and Glasgow. Other commercial aspects of this neighbourhood included grey limestone, lime hearth stone, building stone, a fine quality of silver sand from Godstone, and hard brown building stone from Tilburstow, beyond Godstone. Caterham was principally noted for its yellow and white gravel, and for a good quality red brick earth. From a commercial point of view, therefore, there were some hopes of good traffic. The fact that the terminus lay 1½ miles from its principal source of revenue was, no doubt, a contributory cause of its early failure.

The first mention of the Caterham Railway appears in a letter from

[1]Population (with Warlingham) in 1952 was nearly 30,000. The 1981 census (taking into account altered boundaries etc.) was officially quoted as over 33,000.

the London, Brighton & South Coast Railway[1] to the South-Eastern Railway in 1853:

'Sir, 21st October 1853

The Directors of this Company have been applied to by parties promoting a branch Railway from Godstone Road Station to Caterham, to give their consent to that line.

Under the existing amicable relations with your Company, my Directors do not wish to take any step with regard to the line in question without consulting your Board.

My Directors are informed by the promoters that the Directors of the South-Eastern Company are not opposed to the line, and if so, my Directors are equally prepared not to oppose it, though declining for the present to enter into any further engagements.

I may add that the solicitor, Mr. Sutton, and the engineer, Mr. Hood, of this Company, have been requested to act in their respective capacities for the branch in question.

If it be clearly understood that this would give no umbrage to the Directors of your Company, and would not be construed as a pledge of any engagement between the branch company and ours, my Directors would leave it to these gentlemen to act as they think fit, but unless this be so, they would be requested to decline the offer.

I shall be glad, therefore, to hear from you whether your Board have any feeling on the subject.

I am, Sir,

Your obedient Servant,
SAML. SLIGHT
for the Secretary

G.S. HERBERT, Esq.,
Secretary,
South-Eastern Railway
Company.'

Now what could have been kinder or more honest? The Brighton, whose sense of charity did not always extend towards the Caterham Railway in the same way, was at pains to keep on the right footing with the South-Eastern: for the 'amicable relations' referred to were frequently strained to bursting point.

The South-Eastern Board clearly took umbrage, and had a very definite feeling on the subject, for they replied within a week. Admittedly the letter began 'Sir,' and ended 'I am, Sir, your obedient Servant,' but in between these formal expressions was the underlying cantankerous method of approach so sadly noticeable in the South-Eastern's attitude to its neighbours. The 'amicable relationship' is often to be found in this correspondence, and particularly after one of the more vitriolic attacks hurled by the Brighton and South-Eastern at each other's heads. They did not love one another.

[1] *Relations between the Brighton and South-Eastern Companies,* published by the SER, 1860.

What the answer really implied was that, in accordance with the Agreement of 1848, Caterham lay in South-Eastern territory – which was true – and that if the proposed line was built, the South-Eastern should have the job of taking on its traffic to London from the junction at Godstone Road, though the letter continued rather superciliously, that 'if the Brighton Company carried the traffic, a proper allowance should, of course, be made to them for doing so.' Of course!

The Brighton Directors, who probably considered that the South-Eastern people were rather a common lot, merely replied with a dignified note on the following day that its solicitor and engineer would be asked to abstain from acting for the Caterham Railway.

The South-Eastern, although claiming correctly that Caterham lay in its territory, adopted a bullying attitude that was quite unnecessary. The Brighton was concerned only with the request that a line from Caterham might be allowed to join its line at the disused Godstone Road station, and not with the question of which company should take forward the traffic. Godstone Road had been a Brighton station, and the only stations on that company's line at which the South-Eastern was, by agreement, permitted to stop were those between Croydon and London. It was obvious from the start that there was going to be trouble.

Despite agreements, the South-Eastern and Brighton distrusted each other, and the South-Eastern particularly was always on tenterhooks that the Brighton would find some excuse to penetrate into its territory. The Caterham Railway was, of course, one of those opportunities whereby it could, by purchasing that line, extend towards Tunbridge Wells. The fact that this would not have been playing the game is of no importance, as neither side took much notice of agreements.

Meanwhile, the Caterham Company, unaware of the thundery atmosphere gathering around it, cheerfully went on with its plans. It entered into voluminous correspondence, both with the South-Eastern and the Brighton, especially over the questions of mode of junction with the Brighton and the re-erection of Godstone Road station. These problems are enlarged upon later, but, by their incessant bickering, the main line companies managed to delay the opening of the branch by a whole year.

The Caterham Railway Act received the Royal Assent on 16 June 1854.[1] The Directors, it said, 'were to have a common seal'; this is reproduced on p. 80.

There were forty-two different sections to the Act. 'The Railway', it was stated, 'shall commence at or near the Godstone-road station of

[1]17 and 18 Vic., cap. 68.

the London, Brighton & South Coast Railway, in the parish of Coulsdon . . . and terminate at or near a certain field usually known as Hither North Dean, in the parish of Caterham.' This quaint name was a field-name, situated exactly where the station now is, and is marked on the Rowed map of Caterham of 1736.[1]

The Company was further instructed to erect and maintain a station or lodge where the railway crossed a road on the level, and if it failed to do so, was liable to a fine of £20, and to a penalty of £10 for every day thereafter that the offence continued. There was only one level crossing carrying a public road, that at Salmons Lane, by which stood the Whyteleafe South station.[2] Whyteleafe Hill was not then in use for wheeled traffic, and was only an occupation crossing. The station here was not opened until 1900, although a goods siding existed in the 'sixties.[3]

In Section 23 of the Act the company was informed that it 'must not interfere with the London, Brighton & South Coast Railway, or to take its property, or to construct any railways or branch railways across it either on the level or otherwise.' This clause was inserted at the request of the Brighton, probably (although naturally it did not say so) with an eye to repulsing any attempts on the part of the recalcitrant South-Eastern, which would have had no hesitation in interfering, given the opportunity.

The Caterham Railway was to be completed within three years of the passing of the Act.

On 3 November 1854, the Brighton and South-Eastern entered into another agreement, similar to that of 1848, that 'neither Company shall enter into any arrangement with, or give any assistance, direct or indirect, to any new Company in the district defined by the Agreement of 1848, without the previous consent of the other Company.' The suggestion for this Agreement originated with the Brighton, which remarked, 'For instance, the Brighton Company shall not enter into any Agreement with the Farnborough Company, nor the South-Eastern Company with the Portsmouth Railway Company, without such previous consent as aforesaid.' The astute Brighton was obviously referring, in veiled terms, to the Caterham Railway. By this time, the South-Eastern was turning a baleful glare on other possible competitors, and was inclined to overlook the Caterham. Anyway, it accepted the Agreement without finding fault.

The first meeting of the Caterham Railway Company was called for 21 June 1854, but there was an insufficient number of shareholders to form a quorum, so the meeting was adjourned until 11 November, but no one attended except the reporters.[4] The meeting eventually

---

[1]A Map of the Court-Lodge and Red Hall Farms in the Parish of Catterham in the County of Surry belonging unto Henry Rowed, 1736.

[2]Named Warlingham until 1956.

[3]Ordnance Survey, 25 in. to the mile (1st ed.). Surveyed 1867–8,

[4]*Herapath's Journal*, 25 November 1854.

took place on 20 December,[1] at the *Bridge-House* Hotel, London Bridge. It was reported that the contract for making the line had been let to a Mr Ralph Richardson, and that they had already built a row of labourers' cottages at the top of Mount Pleasant at Caterham. These cottages were described as 'temporary', and were pulled down, with some difficulty, several years ago.

The Company had agreed with the principal landowners on favourable terms, but at the date of the Act (16 June), there had been one noteworthy case of opposition. This came from Henry Aglionby, Esq., of Manor Cottage, near Burntwood Bridge, MP for Cockermouth and a barrister-at-law, and so violently opposed to the Bill that he was to have received £1,600 in compensation for his leasehold interest. In addition, the Company had to erect a high wall for a considerable distance between the railway and his house and grounds, form a new carriageway, and build a new lodge. Fortunately, this obstructive gentleman died on 30 August following the Act, and had no issue; the estate was sold to George Parbury, JP, a more benevolent landowner, who had less objection to trains passing so near his front door. George Drew, as a solicitor and a Director of the railway, wisely took on the job of managing the estate temporarily, and obtained reasonable conditions regarding compensation, which involved the company only to the extent of providing a new carriage-road (the road from Warlingham Station now known as The Avenue). It was largely due to Parbury's influence that the Warlingham station was placed in its present curious position, for it is not even on the road to Warlingham village. In return for this favour, he provided – as a gift – 150 acres of his land for building purposes. Beattie reported that, on the opening of the line, this land was to be conveyed to the shareholders, or their nominees, in proportion of one acre to the holder of each twenty shares of original capital, with power to select and take immediate possession of the land, the order of selection to follow the order of the payment of the shares. This acquisition of land for shareholders was described as 'a new factor in railway matters'. The Directors also wanted to encourage passenger traffic – it was certainly necessary – by giving every such resident freeholder or leaseholder a free pass over the railway for 21 years.

Thomas Wright, writing on the Caterham Railway just before it opened,[2] mentions that Sir Morton Peto, and a few enlightened and philanthropic bankers and merchants in London, had selected some acres of land for the purpose of providing their clerks with good country residences at a moderate cost. 'Such generous conduct,' Wright says, 'will repay an early and well-merited harvest in the

[1]Colquhoun had resigned, and Alexander Beattie had become Chairman.
[2]*Guide to the Caterham Railway, near Croydon in Surrey*, 1856.

improved health and longevity of this confidential and overworked class.'

On a cold and overcast morning, 5 March 1855, the ceremony of cutting the first sod took place. Ironically, this occurred close to the late Mr Aglionby's residence, but on land belonging to Sir William Clayton of Marden Park. The ceremony was performed by the Hon. Sidney Campbell Roper Curzon, a son of the 14th Baron Teynham, 'in the presence of a large assemblage of visitors, with the Clergy and many Ladies and Gentlemen of the vicinity.' Mr Curzon said he hoped the blessing of God would rest on them all and on the undertaking. 'Mr. Curzon then, in a dexterous manner' (and probably with frozen fingers) 'drove the shovel into the earth and quickly filled his barrow, wheeled it a short distance, tipped the earth, and returned with it, when he was greeted with enthusiastic cheers.' The reporter, even if grammatically a little unsound, seemed pleased with the proceedings. Several children from the Parish School, and the daughters of Francis Fuller, then set to work digging the new railway.

There followed two 'sumptuous' feasts, one (third-class) for the poor, the old and the young, who were regaled with roast beef and plum pudding by Mr Seal of the *Half Moon* Inn; the other (first-class) for the Directors and their friends at Manor Cottage, a proceeding that no doubt seriously annoyed the spirit of Mr Aglionby. Beattie, the Chairman, 'proposed the usual loyal toasts in a feeling and impressive manner,' reported *The Railway Times*, but *Herapath's Journal* said he 'delighted everyone present by his kindness and urbanity.' The Reverend Mr Jellicoe (a Caterham man who was Curate at Weybridge) spoke for the clergy, and said that Caterham had hitherto gone by the name of the 'Backwoods', and hoped it would do so no longer. The Chairman then toasted success to the Caterham Railway and coupled with it (wisely, perhaps) the health of the contractor, who was only plain Mister, whereas William McCandlish, the engineer, was Esquire. A toast to the Secretary of the company was not forgotten. The poor man deserved it, for his salary was only £78 7*s.* 6*d.* a year, and he probably had more work to do than anyone else.[1]

At a meeting on 2 July 1855, it was reported that a further contract for construction had been made with Messrs. Furness and Fernandez for £19,000, most of which they never received, as will be seen later. The Engineer reported that up to 1 June, 15,000 cubic yards of earth had been excavated, half of the permanent fencing erected, and one of the two overbridges had been started. A further 90,000 cubic yards of earth had yet to be dealt with, one more bridge, several culverts and the stations built, and yet he was able to say that the line would

[1]From reports in *Herapath's Journal* and *The Railway Times*, 10 March 1855.

be ready for opening on 21 September following. It is remarkable to add that this did, in fact, turn out to be correct. It was only the haggling of the Brighton and South-Eastern that prevented the opening.

It was intended in 1855 (plans were deposited in November of that year) to extend southwards by two branches, the one to the 'Quarries at Upwood,'[1] and the other along the Harestone valley to War Coppice Quarry. On the latter branch, the gradients were to be 1 in 56, 82½, 60, 37, 30 and 10. Though the last-mentioned figure was only for a distance of about 1½ furlongs, it is not to be supposed that the Board of Trade would ever have sanctioned such a line for passengers. Neither branch went further than the paper stage. At this time, the Godstone Quarry Company sent 55 tons of stone to London daily at 15s. a ton. Tupwood Quarry claimed to be sending 50,000 tons of fire and building-stone away annually. From an investigation by the Caterham Railway in 1855, it was estimated that takings by the railway would amount to £30,000 a year.

When the Directors of the Caterham Company applied to Parliament for the original Act, the Brighton requested them to apply for an extension northwards to join the Croydon & Epsom Railway near Wallington.[2] 'This,' the Chairman reported, 'would give the residents in the vicinity [of Caterham] the advantage of availing themselves of the frequent trains (being at present 65 daily) running upon the Croydon & Epsom Railway, which line will also give to the district the advantage of a West-end terminus in London, by means of the West-End & Crystal Palace Railway, and the Wimbledon & Croydon Railway, now both in course of construction.'

Plans were prepared for the line, which was to run from 'Hayslanebridge' (at Kenley), thence under the Brighton main line a short distance south of Purley station. The Brighton claimed that, by this means, it could provide the Caterham Company with 'better facilities and greater accommodation in the frequency of transit.'

Although they did not say so, the Brighton, by building a spur from the main line, would have had a spare line to London; more important still, half of the Caterham Company would have been on the west side of the main line, and therefore in Brighton territory, which would have upset all the Agreements with the South-Eastern. But the Brighton changed its mind again and, in 1855 requested the Caterham to build a separate bridge over the Godstone Road – which was not required by the original Act – at a cost of £2,006. Even when this was done, the 'greater accommodation' was still withheld and was later one of the matters brought up in a court case.

In May 1855, trouble began over the method of junction with the

[1] i.e. Tupwood, near Godstone Hill.

[2] This would have obviated any necessity for the Caterham to make a junction at Godstone Road station.

Brighton. The Caterham Company wrote to the South-Eastern, asking for their assent to the proposed junction (as agreed by the Brighton) and boldly asking for £700 towards expenses. Any opportunity for disagreeing with or annoying the Brighton always seemed to result in a quick reply from the South-Eastern, who maintained that it was not for them to assent to the mode of junction, adding unkindly that they had not sufficient interest in the Caterham Railway to justify a contribution of £700. 'It is premature,' they said, 'to take any part in the operations of the Caterham Railway until it is settled what benefit this Company is to receive from the traffic; and what portion of the working arrangements are to be carried by us, with the consent of the Brighton.'

A month later, the Caterham Railway submitted proposals for an arrangement whereby the South-Eastern would work the line. Unfortunately, the Minutes do not reveal what these proposals were. The South-Eastern, making legal enquiries, found that they were empowered to enter into a working arrangement, but had no power to purchase without an Act of Parliament. The proposals, therefore, were not acceptable to them, and they declined to show any interest. Nevertheless, they had sufficient interest to open negotiations with the Brighton as to the expected traffic from the Caterham line, the provision for stoppage of South-Eastern trains at the junction, and the mode of junction itself. The Caterham Company was not included in these negotiations – not officially, at any rate, though there can be little doubt that the news filtered through. Caterham was soon made aware of the objectionable habits of its neighbours.

At a joint Brighton-South Eastern meeting on 7 July 1855, Captain Barlow, the South-Eastern Superintendent, reported that a through crossing from the Caterham Railway to the Brighton would be possible if the Board found it acceptable. The Brighton seemed to have no objection, provided the Caterham paid for any land used in making the junction.

Caterham, finding the South-Eastern unhelpful, turned its attention to the Brighton, and asked how much would be charged for letting them run through to London Bridge, or even for picking up the traffic at the Caterham Junction. This request was read at the Brighton Company's Board Meeting on 30 August 1855, the somewhat surprising and confusing resolution being passed to 'put off the above, but that Craven [*the Locomotive Superintendent*] be authorised to supply to the contractors of the Caterham Railway, a Ballast Engine, upon the Caterham Railway paying a proper remuneration.'

It was not until 22 November that Caterham reminded the Brighton about their request for rates and charges from the junction to London, to which the Brighton replied, with a brevity amounting to rudeness:

'We have no station at the junction, and this Company's charges for passengers from Stoat's Nest are: 1st class 3/-; 2nd class 2/3; 3rd class 1/6.' With a foot-tapping South-Eastern scowling away in the near background, it is perhaps surprising that the Brighton did not attempt to woo any company, however small, into a state of total alliance.

A month later they were still arguing, the Brighton prosecuting its delaying action with vigour. Jacomb-Hood, the Brighton engineer, reported that 'laying in a set of leading points from the Down line at Godstone Road might be done without danger,' whereupon the Caterham was informed that if it paid for the entire expenses of works and the wages of a signalman, the points would be put in.

It was obvious that the Brighton could, or would, deal with only one point at a time, and it was not until 16 January 1856 that the Caterham Company requested permission to erect passenger platforms at Godstone Road. To this, the Brighton passed a resolution to ask the South-Eastern, an incomprehensible decision, as it was Brighton property.[1] Whether they really did so is not known – there is certainly no report on it, and it was probably only another means of fobbing off the Caterham people while the Brighton tried to think. In February, they informed Caterham that 'it would be inadvisable to have a station at the junction . . . as its proximity to Stoat's Nest would cause great impediment to the traffic on the main line' (a familiar phrase) 'and that the only way would be to move Stoat's Nest to the point of junction, without cost to the Brighton, who must be allowed to retain all traffic appertaining to that station.'

The Caterham Company was beginning to despair of ever opening the line and had, in the meantime, been making renewed overtures to the South-Eastern, who suggested terms of working similar to those proposed to the Mid-Kent Railway, then in course of construction:

1. The Caterham Company to complete the line with proper stations, signals and sidings, before it opened.
2. All works required for extension of traffic after the line opened to be done at the cost of the Caterham Company.
3. Junction to be made to the satisfaction of the South-Eastern Company's Engineer.
4. South-Eastern to provide staff, and plant for working the line, and to maintain the permanent way at expiration of two years from opening; meanwhile the Caterham Company to maintain it.
5. During the first two years a sum of 40 per cent. to be deducted from gross receipts, to be retained by the South-Eastern for working expenses.

[1]But they were touchy where the SE was concerned. At a Joint LBSC and SE meeting on 17 January 1856, the Brighton directors 'expressed surprise' that the SE had agreed to work the Caterham, without first consulting them.

6. After the South-Eastern take over, amount deducted to be raised to 50 per cent.
7. Caterham Company to fix all rates and fares to and from all Caterham Railway stations and London.

On 28 February 1856, the Caterham Company wrote declining the terms of working, and at the South-Eastern Board Meeting on 6 March, a resolution was passed (apparently ignoring the letter from Caterham) 'to communicate with the Caterham Company as to supply of such engines, carriages and trucks as they may require.'

In May, the South-Eastern submitted a new agreement for working, on the terms of the Caterham Company repaying the actual cost of working, plus 10 per cent. for depreciation of working stock. Sir Morton Peto, the London financier, who had considerable interest in the Caterham Railway, and had already had an interview with Eborall, the new South-Eastern General Manager, did not approve of the new proposals, and wrote to say that 'further negotiations with him may be considered at an end.' Some people knew how to deal with the South-Eastern.

On 2 June 1856 the Caterham wrote to the South-Eastern that they proposed to open the line at the beginning of August, and asked to be supplied with engine and carriages as the South-Eastern had earlier suggested. Unfortunately, the South-Eastern, no doubt still feeling nettled by Sir Morton Peto's attitude, had by now reversed their opinion. They wrote that, on the advice of the Locomotive Superintendent, 'the present engine power was short of the actual necessities of South-Eastern traffic.' They were not, therefore, in a position to supply anything.

Consequently, the Caterham Company had to start all over again in an attempt to flirt successfully with the Brighton. The Board of Trade had sanctioned the opening of the line, and the Brighton were asked for the times of their trains which could be stopped at the junction 'to make arrangements for forwarding such traffic in carriages to be provided by the Caterham Railway.' Even at this eleventh hour the Caterham was determined to get engines and rolling-stock from somewhere, and run them through to London. The Brighton, who obviously just did not want to bother with the matter at all, replied that the request was unreasonable, and excused themselves on the grounds of 'public safety'. However, somewhat mollified by the Caterham's hint that the South-Eastern would not play properly, the Brighton agreed at the next Board Meeting (21 July) to move Stoat's Nest to the junction at a cost (to Caterham, of course) of £100. In actual fact, this was not done, and at the time of opening there was nothing at the junction except a couple of derelict platforms. After the opening, minutes were still passing to and fro between the Brighton and South-Eastern on the question of who was going to build the station. The Caterham Company wrote volumes of letters to both companies – six of them in a week during the peak period. Stoat's Nest was still open, and the Brighton refused to keep two stations going, intimating that they would have to close Stoat's Nest. At this, the Rev. George Randolph, of Coulsdon, foolishly suggested they should make a station half-way between Stoat's Nest and Godstone Road, which would have been useless to Caterham passengers. Even George Hawkins, the Brighton Manager, said at a Board Meeting on 7 August that there was 'urgent necessity for some further accommodation at Godstone Road'. Nothing further was mentioned about trains stopping to connect until the Board Meeting ten days later, and only a few days before the Caterham line opened, when the Brighton agreed to stop four Up and four Down trains on weekdays and three on Sundays at the junction. Even this was altered at the last moment, as the South-Eastern, apparently annoyed at being left out of the picture, demanded that two of their trains should stop.

Craven was ordered to supply 'an engine and two or three carriages' for working the line, as McCandlish, the Engineer of the Caterham Company, said Sir Morton Peto had made arrangements to hire the plant from the Brighton, a fact denied by Sir Morton a few days later, saying that he had authorised nothing of the sort and declining to be a party to it! With such internal strife and continuous difficulties over hiring the plant, it is not surprising that the opening of the line had been delayed a year.

The *Railway Times*, in its pre-opening notice of the Caterham Railway, indirectly commented on the main lines' controversy, and showed some disapproval of their behaviour towards such a small and inoffensive line. 'After a twelve month delay,' it said, 'in effecting arrangements between the Brighton and South-Eastern, this short line of about four miles and a half is to be opened to the public on Monday.[1] The space of time between completion and opening would be inexplicable, but for the awkward "political" situation in which the Caterham is placed. It lies in the South-Eastern territory, but opens on the Brighton. The remarkable tenderness that has existed between these two Companies on the subject must no doubt be peculiarly gratifying to their shareholders, in so far as it displays a determination on the part of both not to enter into any agreement that may be unpleasant to either. But the Caterham has been suffering in the meantime, and, it appears to us, has obtained but scant justice, and certainly no liberality in the end . . . The fares appear excessive, when compared with other branch traffic in the neighbourhood. The local charges are, of course, more moderate.'

[1]4 August. Public service began the following day.

The fares from Caterham to London Bridge, which included the main line companies' tolls, were: 1st class, 3*s*. 4*d*.; 2nd class, 2*s*. 10*d*.; 3rd class, 2*s*. 1*d*.; Parliamentary, 1*s*. 6*d*. This was a heavy price to pay for 18 miles, especially when one remembers that a penny bought so much more in 1856 than even in 1939. The comparative fares to, for instance, Epsom (18½ miles from London Bridge) were: 1st class, 2*s*. 6*d*.; 2nd class, 2*s*.; 3rd class or Parliamentary, 1*s*. 6*d*.

Parliamentary, or Government, fares had been introduced in 1844 by Gladstone, who thought that the lowest class of passenger was entitled to a little more consideration. This Act gave them legal status, and a limited amount of comfort. Hitherto, they had been carried in trucks, and fully exposed to the vagaries of the English climate, and smoke from the engine; and they were packed in like sardines, though there was some difference in the way they were packed. Parliamentary trains were to run once a day in each direction, calling at all stations; there were to be attached closed carriages with seats; and the charge was not to exceed one penny per mile. A speed of not less than 12 miles per hour had to be maintained by these trains, and the Board of Trade had the right to amend the schedules if necessary.

It was announced by the Caterham Company that they would be enabled, by the assistance of the Brighton and South-Eastern Companies, to issue season tickets to and from London and Caterham for ten years, at £7 per annum first-class, and £5 per annum second-class, to persons building houses on the property of the Company.[1] One cannot help feeling that there must have been some catch in these astonishingly low figures, for someone must have had to pay the main line companies' toll. Perhaps the cost of the 'good country residences at a moderate cost' was less moderate for those who wished to have a season.

Three Directors and three Officers of the company required passes to London, and the Secretary (George Mill) asked the Brighton if they would issue them between the Caterham Junction and London, which the Brighton agreed to do – for £18 a ticket.

A bill announcing the opening of the line ran as follows:

OPENING of the CATERHAM
RAILWAY

NOTICE is hereby given, That on and after TUESDAY next, the 5th AUGUST, the Caterham Railway will be OPEN for Passengers and Goods in conjunction with the London and Brighton and South-Eastern Railway Companies.

For Times of Starting, and Arrival of Trains, Fares, &c., &c., see "Bradshaw," Hand-Bills.

By Order of the Bard (*sic*)
GEORGE MILL, Secretary.

Caterham Railway Company, Hibernia Chambers,
London-bridge, August 1, 1856.

[1]The 1952 rate for a third-class season between London Bridge and Caterham was £35 11*s*. 0*d*. per annum. This does not, however, necessitate one's building a house there. The comparable 1985 figure is £699, or £197 a quarter.

Chapter Four

Opening of the Caterham Railway

The formal opening took place on Monday, 4 August 1856, when a special train, with Directors and their friends, 'left the London Bridge Station at a quarter past twelve o'clock, arriving at Caterham at about one o'clock.'[1] The party included Brighton and South-Eastern officers, Colonel Carruthers, Mr Mechi, the Sheriff-elect, and Mr Alderman and Sheriff Rose.

There is no evidence that the occasion was heralded by the bands, flags and bunting that generally marked the opening of a new line, but the usual 'cold collation', furnished by the London Tavern, took place at the new hotel. Mr Francis Fuller, now Chairman, presided, and various loyal and other toasts were given and responded to.No doubt it was as sumptuous a feast as that given at the sod-cutting revelry the previous year; for whatever the financial state or prospects of a railway company, they never failed to eat and drink sufficiently well to cause the newspapers to comment that 'the proceedings were concluded in a satisfactory manner.'[2]

Another report[3] gives a more lively description of the opening. 'The party on the special train . . . were met by the whole population, headed by one of the goodly specimens of the farming interest in the county – a Mr. Smith,[4] a gentleman of some 20 stone weight, who is a practical illustration of the proverb "laugh and grow fat" . . . Messrs. Fuller and Smith conducted the Company round the country, diversifying the enjoyment by occasional sojourns at improvised halting-places where, by a careful forethought, iced champagne and other agreeables had been provided.' Contemporary reports all indicate that the weather was fine and very hot.

There later followed a *déjeuner* or *fête champêtre* in a marquee on Mr Fuller's lawn, 'where that stalwart franklin, Mr. Smith, sang some capital songs.'

The Directors stated that they could supply stone in London for 6*s*. 6*d*. a ton, maintaining thereby that masonry walls would be reduced to about £6 a rod instead of about £15 a rod, as for brick. Unfortunately, their hopes were never realised.

The opening proceedings were marred by the fact that Caterham's much-loved Rector, James Legrew, was dying, and did in fact pass away the following day, the first day that a regular passenger service ran. It was, perhaps, fortunate that he did not die just before the formal opening, for the locals might then have been torn between a funeral – and an important one – and the novelty of a railway opening.

---

[1]*Illustrated London News*, 9 August 1856.
[2]*Ibid*.
[3]*Railway Record*, 9 August 1856.
[4]Alfred Smith, of Tupwood, one of the original Directors.

An engraving of Caterham station from the *Illustrated London News* dated 9 August 1856. It is standing on the field of Hither North Dean, with Waller Lane on the left leading up the hill to Caterham village. The building on the left is the Railway Hotel, while the one on the right is the stable accommodation. The smallest building, in the centre, is the station.

Another view of Caterham station of the 1860s. The top-hatted policeman and the P.O. wagon 'Clay Cross 380' are worthy of inspection.

So the line was at last open – but only just. There were, according to the time-table, to be four trains each way daily, and three each way on Sundays. On weekdays, two connexions were made by the Brighton, and two by the South-Eastern.

The Brighton connexions worked in satisfactorily, and the through journey to London Bridge was performed in 45–50 minutes. The South-Eastern, however, was a little vague. There certainly were two of their trains labelled as setting down for the Caterham branch, but as one of these arrived forty minutes after the branch train had left, it did not seem of much use. On Sundays, the South-Eastern thoughtfully stopped the 8.10 am (originally fast to Redhill) when one waited about two and a half hours at the junction for the branch train.

The timings on the branch were not so much vague as idiotic. Two minutes only was allowed between the present Purley and Kenley, although this involved 1 mile 18 chains of a steady up gradient of 1 in 422; an average speed of over 30 mph, which sounds highly improbable. Trains running downhill to the junction were allowed five minutes. Five minutes was allowed between Kenley and Warlingham, where the gradient was 1 in 160 for one mile, followed by just over a mile at 1 in 118, and eight minutes from there to Caterham, but as this last section included a considerable distance at 1 in 90, it is perhaps not to be wondered at (*see gradient profile on page 87*).

Construction of the line had not presented many difficulties. It was, of course, single throughout, and remained so until the end of the century. A fairly deep cutting round the curve from Purley, and less extensive ones at Kenley, and at Burntwood Bridge (between Warlingham and Caterham) constituted the only major earthworks. At Kenley and Burntwood-lane, too, were the only bridges, both over the line. The overbridge in Purley cutting, known as Byron's Bridge, was not erected until 1870 (by agreement with the landowner) and was reconstructed in 1916–17.

Some writers, e.g. *Clinker's Register*, maintain the Brighton Railway changed the name of Godstone Road to Caterham Junction on the Caterham Railway opening, but the Caterham Company's own timetable of October 1856 (*see page* 36) shows it as Godstone Road, and the Brighton referred to it as that in correspondence in September 1856 (*see page* 39). Anyway, the South-Eastern, who had a natural disinclination to do anything the Brighton did, persisted in calling it by its original name until the following January.

In 1905,[1] an elderly gentleman described the early Godstone Road as having been a single platform with a rough shed for passengers (which may have meant a single platform on either side of the line, or some kind of early 'island' platform). There was a high mast-like

[1]*Railway Magazine*, Vol. XVI, p. 346.

With old and new signal-boxes showing in top left-hand corner, two sets of starter signals, and advertising signs recently removed from fence, it is possible that this photograph of Caterham old station was taken on 31 December 1899, the last day of its active life. The new station was opened alongside the next day.

Sleepers and rails being unloaded near Caterham, for work on doubling the line in the late 1890s. *Courtesy Batsford Books*

erection at the south end of the platform – the semaphore signal post. He adds that the later name of Caterham Junction was a source of criticism, as it was a frequent occurrence for passengers to alight from the main line train under the impression they were at Caterham, descend some 'perilously steep steps' by the side of the arch into the road, and then see the Caterham train steaming away round the curve. It would appear that staff arrangements were rather hazy, but it is doubtful if, in those far-off days, the Brighton would have paid the wages of a station-master for the sake of the Caterham Railway. It is even more doubtful whether the Caterham Railway would have had any money to pay any wages to anyone. The only indication of the existence of Purley, apart from two or three cottages, was in Purley House, the late residence of John Horne Tooke. He wrote of it in *The Diversions of Purley*.

Caterham Junction was re-named Purley on 1 October 1888. Inhabitants of Purley had petitioned the Brighton to change the name at an earlier date, but the petition was refused. The Post Office then took up the matter, for mail destined for Purley had often been sent to Caterham, and *vice versa*.[1]

Kenley was called Coulsdon until December 1856. The station was in the parish of Coulsdon, and Kenley, though an old name, was not then a place; the present station name was taken from Kenley House, where Drew lived until he moved to Caterham. The down side station-house here is the original building (apart from some alterations of 1876) designed by Richard Whittall, of Abingdon Street, Westminster, in what he called the Old English style of Domestic Architecture.[2] There may have always been an up platform and passing loop here, for in 1871 it was reported that a Booking Office was wanted 'on the up platform at Kenley at a cost of £140.'[3]

Thomas Wright, in his tour of the line, noted 'the fine sweep of Riddles Down, with its carpet of green sward, speckled with innumerable little groups of dark shrubs.' Despite the extensive building in the neighbourhood, the scene remains the same today. Legend has it that the yews on these downs were planted (in the days when archery had not been superseded by firearms) in order to supply material for bows.

Whyteleafe did not exist. The White Leaf field, so called from the aspens growing in it, was bought about 1856 by a Mr Glover, who built a house there and called it Whyte Leaf, the 'y' presumably being regarded as a superior substitute for 'i'. There was always a signal-box at 'White-leaf Crossing'. The original one was destroyed by fire on the night of 22 October 1867.

[1]Resker: *History and Development of Purley*.

[2]Mr Hamilton Ellis thinks Whittall may have been the architect for some of the stations on the Redhill-Guildford line, which are of a similar type.

[3]No building shown on the up side on Ordnance Survey, 25 in. map, 1867–8.

CATERHAM RAILWAY

(In Connection with the London & Brighton & South Eastern Railways.)

THE FOLLOWING TRAINS WILL RUN DURING THE MONTH OF OCTOBER AND UNTIL FURTHER NOTICE :—

DOWN.	WEEK DAYS.							SUNDAYS.						FARES FROM LONDON. Single Tickets.				Return.	
	a.m.	a.m.	a.m.	p.m.	p.m.	p.m.		a.m.	a.m.	a.m.	p.m.	p.m.							
BRIGHTON .... dep.	..	..	..	..	..	6 30	..	..	8 30	..	..	6 30	..						
DOVER .... „	..	..	..	..	..	..	..	..	..	..	..	..	..						
	..	Dorking. 7 55	Hayward's Heath. 9 15	..	..	..	..	..	..	..	..	..	..						
	Brighton Station. 1, 2, P.	1, 2, 3.	S. E. Station. 1 & 2.	Brighton Station. 1, 2, 3.	S. E. Station. 1 & 2.	1, 2, 3.		Brighton Station. 1, 2, P.	1, 2, 3	Brighton Station. 1 & 2	Brighton Station. 1, 2, 3.	1, 2, P.		1st Class. s. d.	2nd Class. s. d.	3rd Class. s. d.	Parl. s. d.	1st Class. s. d.	2nd Class. s. d.
LONDON BRIDGE...... dep.	6 0	..	9 30	3 0	5 30	..	..	7 0	..	10 45	6 0	..	..						
New Cross .... „	6 5	..	..	3 5	..	..	..	7 5	..	10 50	6 5	..	..						
Forest Hill .... „	6 15	..	..	3 15	..	..	..	7 13	..	..	..	..	..						
Croydon (East) .... „	6 25	..	9 54	3 25	5 54	..	..	7 25	..	11 10	6 25	..	..						
Caterham Junction ...... „	6 35	8 35	10 5	3 35	6 5	8 6	..	7 35	10 15	11 20	6 35	8 15	..	2 6	2 0	1 6	1 1	4 0	3 0
Coulsdon...................... „	6 37	8 37	10 7	3 37	6 7	8 7	..	7 37	10 17	11 22	6 37	8 17	..	2 9	2 3	1 10	1 2	4 2	3 5
Warlingham .... „	6 42	8 42	10 12	3 42	6 12	8 12	..	7 42	10 22	11 27	6 42	8 22	..	3 0	2 6	2 0	1 4	4 6	3 9
CATERHAM.............. arr.	6 50	8 50	10 20	3 50	6 20	8 20	..	7 50	10 30	11 35	6 50	8 30	..	3 4	2 10	2 1	1 6	5 0	4 3

An Omnibus leaves Caterham for Godstone, Oxted, Limpsfield, and Westerham, every Evening, except Sundays, on the arrival of the 5.30 p.m. Down Train.
Parcels forwarded to all parts of London.

UP.	WEEK DAYS.							SUNDAYS.						FARES FROM CATERHAM. Single Tickets.				Return.	
	1, 2, P. a.m.	1, 2, 3. a.m.	1 & 2. a.m.	1, 2, 3. p.m.	1 & 2. p.m.	1, 2, 3. p.m.		1, 2, P. a.m.	1, 2, 3. a.m.	1 & 2 a.m.	1, 2, 3. p.m.	1, 2, P. p.m.		s. d.	s. d.	s. d.	s. d.	s. d.	s. d.
CATERHAM.............. dep.	6 15	8 15	9 50	3 15	5 5	7 45	..	7 15	9 50	11 0	6 15	7 50	..	..	..	..	..	..	..
Warlingham .... „	6 20	8 20	9 55	3 20	5 10	7 50	..	7 20	9 55	11 5	6 20	7 55	..	0 4	0 3	0 2	0 1	..	..
Coulsdon...................... „	6 25	8 25	10 0	3 25	5 15	7 55	..	7 25	10 0	11 10	6 25	8 0	..	0 8	0 6	0 4	0 3	..	..
Caterham Junction ...... „	6 30	8 30	10 5	3 30	5 20	8 0	..	7 30	10 10	11 15	6 30	8 10	..	0 10	0 8	0 6	0 4	..	..
Croydon (East) .... „	..	8 37	10 15	..	5 29	8 13	..	..	10 20	..	..	8 20	..	1 5	1 1	0 10	0 8	2 0	1 6
Forest Hill .... „	..	8 51	10 20	..	5 47	8 24	..	..	10 30	..	..	8 30	..	2 3	1 9	1 3	1 0	3 4	2 7
New Cross .... „	..	..	..	..	..	8 35	..	..	10 40	..	..	8 40	..	2 9	2 2	1 6	1 3	4 1	3 3
LONDON BRIDGE...... arr.	..	9 0	10 35	..	6 0	8 50	..	..	11 0	..	..	9 0	..	3 4	2 10	2 1	1 6	5 0	4 3
BRIGHTON .... arr.	8 20	..	..	5 35	..	..	..	9 20	..	12 40	8 20	..	..						
DOVER .... „		.	1 30	..	9 30	..	..	..	..	..	..	..	..						

Passengers to and from the Stations on the Caterham Railway change carriages at the Caterham Junction.

SEASON TICKETS.

STATIONS.	FARES. First Class.			Second Class.		
	£	s.	d.	£	s.	d.
CATERHAM TO LONDON	18	0	0	15	6	0
WARLINGHAM TO LONDON......	16	0	0	13	12	0
COULSDON TO LONDON	14	0	0	11	18	0

When Two Members of the same Family, being relatives, residing under the same roof, subscribe for Annual Tickets, a reduction at the rate of 10 per Cent. will be allowed; when Three Members subscribe, 15 per Cent.; and when Four or more Members subscribe, 20 per Cent., upon condition that such Tickets commence from the same day, and are for the same period.

Caterham Railway Company, Hibernia Chambers, London Bridge, *October*, 1856.

To Builders and others.—With a view to encourage the erection of buildings of a residential character in the Caterham Valley, the Directors of the Caterham Railway are prepared to facilitate those operations in the following manner. For each house of the annual value of £50 and upwards, a First Class Ticket will be issued, for seven years, and for each house of the annual value of £30 and upwards, a Second Class Ticket will be issued, as under. The conditions on which these Tickets will be granted may be obtained on application to the Secretary.

STATIONS.	FARES. First Class.			Second Class.		
	£	s.	d.	£	s.	d.
CATERHAM to LONDON..	6	0	0	5	2	0
WARLINGHAM to LONDON	5	6	8	4	10	8
COULSDON to LONDON	4	13	4	3	19	4

By order of the Board,

Geo. Mill, *Secretary*.

An Omnibus leaves Westerham for Caterham at 8.0, to meet the 9.50 Up Train, and leaves Caterham for Westerham on the arrival of the 5.30 Down Train.
... from Westerham to Caterham 1*s*. 6*d*. Inside, and 1*s*. Outside. Return Tickets 2*s*. 3*d*. Inside, and 1*s*. 6*d*. Outside.
Oxted to Caterham 1*s*. Inside, and 9*d*. Outside. Godstone to Caterham 8*d*. Inside, and 6*d*. Outside.

Waterlow & Sons, Printers, Carpenters' Hall, London Wall.

The first published time-table of the Caterham Railway.

Warlingham station was rebuilt during the first half of 1862 at a cost of £274 2*s*. 10*d*.[1] The stationmaster's house is still in existence on the up side, with a piece of South-Eastern type awning over the doors. The signal-box here, as at Kenley, was erected in 1875, at a cost of £90. Some years ago, consideration was given to moving the station half a mile nearer Caterham, by the Burntwood Bridge, but the matter was dropped.

A short distance beyond Burntwood Bridge is Half Moon Crossing (now a footbridge) perpetuating the name of the old coaching inn which was situated close to the line here, at the junction of the Lewes road and the old road that ran steeply over Tillingdown. It is not known when it ceased to be an inn – probably through the falling-off of road traffic, but it is presumed to have been finally demolished in the late 1890s, when the railway track was doubled.

The original Caterham station (*see page* 32) was built in the same style as Kenley, although it was larger, and further enlarged towards the end of 1862. Until recently there remained a small portion of the platform, and the goods shed, which had originally been used as the engine shed. There were a fair number of sidings in the goods yard, with reasonable docking for coal. The whole yard has gone now, and in its place is, of course, a supermarket. Caterham 'new' station is now sandwiched insignificantly between the supermarket and a high bank; such is progress.

Ordnance Maps of the 'sixties show mileposts on both sides of the line (a practice adopted by the Brighton Railway), the distances being marked both from Caterham and from the Junction. As the surveying for these maps was done after the South-Eastern had acquired the line, it must be assumed that these were the original Caterham Railway posts, for the South-Eastern mileposted from London only.

The type of locomotive used in these early days, whether during the two years of the Brighton era, or later under the South-Eastern, is uncertain. The late H.L. Hopwood said he believed two 'Bury' locomotives worked the line, but he gives no authority for the statement.[2] The early photograph of Caterham taken about 1865 (not before), shows a locomotive which Mr Hamilton Ellis thinks is a Sharp standard type of the early 1840s, probably rebuilt from a 2–2–2, with equalised coupled axles – a typical Cudworth arrangement for engines on lightly laid lines. The boiler and front end were unchanged, and characteristic of Sharp's early designs. As rebuilt, the firebox is in the rear of the trailing axle, as on Cudworth's engines used on the Hastings line.

It is possible that the Brighton supplied most of the tickets, luggage labels, dockets and other insignia to be found connected with any

[1]SER Reports and Accounts.
[2]*Railway Magazine*, Vol. XLVIII, p. 143.

railway station. No record of a ticket headed 'Caterham Railway' seems to have been found – not surprising, perhaps, in view of the very few, comparatively speaking, that must have been sold. The company did, however, produce at least one time-sheet, and a poster on goods charges. A month after the original publication of this book, a copy of each was discovered, by chance, in a large volume, thick with dust, in the Solicitor's office at Waterloo.

The Company built two hotels, one at Purley, which was known for many years as the *Caterham Junction*, and one at Caterham, the *Railway*. They were let to tenants, the one at Caterham being held by W.J. Gwynn who was, in addition, a wine and spirit merchant and a builder. The *Railway* at Caterham was pulled down in 1901–2 to make way for shops, and rebuilt in its present atrocious architectural style on an adjacent piece of ground. It was re-named *Valley* Hotel about 1917, and is now no longer even that.

The type of locomotive probably used on the Caterham Railway in its earliest days: Bury tank engine No. 4, rebuilt. *Drawn by C. Hamilton Ellis*

Chapter Five

Trouble with the Main Line Companies

During August and September of 1856 there was an almost ceaseless flow of complaints from the Secretary of the Caterham Company, mostly directed at the Brighton, whose board meetings were nearly always enlivened by some fresh attack.

Caterham wished to issue a season ticket to a Mr Pain between Caterham and East Croydon, but the Brighton said they did not issue seasons between these points (i.e. between the Junction and East Croydon). Immediately came back the reply that Caterham 'intend to issue a season to Mr Pain and are prepared to pay any sum the Brighton Company may demand, and that if the Brighton Company requires the ticket to be taken out to London this [Caterham] Company will pay the difference in distance.'[1] The Brighton flatly refused to issue any season of any description between East Croydon and the Caterham Junction. As it was all their property between these points, it may have been that they had taken a dislike to Mr Pain, or perhaps they were just frightened about what the South-Eastern might have to say in the matter. Whatever the reason, their action can only be described as both malicious and stupid. The Caterham Company merely replied that the train and other arrangements were 'very objectionable' and requested certain alterations in the train service on 1 September. As this letter was written on 28 August, they must have been very optimistic. Needless to say, no alterations were made.

On 8 September came the complaint that Brighton excursions did not call at the junction, and that excursionists from the Caterham district were obliged to walk to and from Stoat's Nest. The Brighton resolved, surprisingly enough, to write to the effect that 'as this Company desires to afford every reasonable facility to the traffic of the Caterham Company, the Sunday Intermediate Main Line Excursions Train on and after 21 September will stop by signal at Godstone Road.'

In general, the service was far from satisfactory, and within a few days there was a further complaint that passengers were inconvenienced and delayed 'by the frequent late arrival of the Brighton Company's 6.30 pm up from Brighton, and that it would be better if the South-Eastern's train due London Bridge at 10.5 pm were stopped instead.' The South-Eastern, when they heard about this, took no notice; the 10.5 was about their only fast train, and they were not going to be gulled into stopping it at a derelict platform for the benefit of the Caterham rustics.

Amongst this agglomeration of complaints appeared, from time to time, letters about the 'junction accommodation'. On one occasion

[1]LB&SCR Minutes, 4 September 1856.

A fine view of a branch train entering Caterham station in 1905. The track layout signalling and signal-box can be clearly seen in this view. The tall chimney on the right was part of the Urban Electric Supply Company Ltd.
Lens of Sutton

'H' Class locomotive hauling a 3-coach set, leaving Purley for Caterham in 1926.
H.C. Casserley

Caterham threatened to remove rails and take down 'one or more signal posts' belonging to the Brighton Company, and deal with the question of platforms themselves. The Brighton bully, now being bullied, and faced with the fact that they might one day find half the rails torn up and bold little men from Caterham making their own arrangements, promptly sent their Engineer to investigate. He reported that all alterations to rails and posts could be done if necessary. It does not appear as if very much *was* done, and in November occurred the first of the two major embroilments in which this unlucky line was involved. In this instance, however, it was the Caterham Railway that took the bull by the horns, and battered its way into court in a fury of resolve to see justice done by its unneighbourly neighbours. This followed a meeting of the Caterham Company, with Francis Fuller in the chair. He explained that he had no reason to doubt that the line would be remunerative if the company was allowed to charge the same fares as the other companies did – referring, of course, to the heavy toll demanded. When it was discovered that the company had been let down by the Brighton over the matter of the extension to the Croydon & Epsom line, and building of Godstone-road bridge (*see page* 25), it decided that the situation was intolerable. One of the Directors, Mr Greig, boldly but tactlessly put his foot in things by announcing that 'by continuing the line from Caterham to Godstone[1] the South-Eastern Company might avoid the angle at Reigate, save five miles in the route to Paris, and escape two tunnels.' This may have been partly true, but it was a rude gesture to the Brighton.

The case was heard on 17 November, in the Court of Common Pleas, Westminster, before Mr Justice Creswell, and created some sensation in the railway world. *Herapath's Journal* described it as having an important bearing on the operation of the Railway Regulation Act.[2]

Sir Fitzroy Kelly, for Caterham, moved for a rule calling on the Brighton and South-Eastern Companies to show cause why a writ of injunction should not be issued against them enjoining them to afford greater facilities and advantages to the Caterham. The Counsel moved on the affidavits of Mr Mill (the Caterham Secretary) and a clergyman (who was unnamed) complaining that the development of the traffic was being obstructed by the Brighton and South-Eastern. These two companies were not interested in the fortunes of the Caterham.

It was argued for the plaintiffs that passengers had been told on the main lines that the stations on the Caterham Railway were 'not known'; and that main line trains did not stop at the Caterham

[1]i.e. Godstone station on the Dover line.

[2]1844, 7 and 8 Vic., cap. 85, 'Statutory Provisions as to cheap trains and fares.'

Junction, although advertised to do so, to the great delay and inconvenience of passengers. This latter point must have been very irritating! Not only was the intending traveller to, say, Warlingham rather in the dark as to his ultimate destination, but was liable to suffer the indignity of having to leap out of a non-stop train at Caterham Junction. They further complained that the starting of trains from London to Caterham was inconvenient, and the trains too few; that the fares were excessive and that no third-class returns were issued; and that there was no station accommodation provided at the junction for waiting passengers 'who were in consequence exposed to the cold and wet'. It was only too evident that what there was of 'Godstone Road' had been re-opened on the cheap. Even today, Purley, from its elevated position, suffers from a certain draughtiness, so the discomforts of the 'fifties can well be imagined. Sir Fitzroy contended that reasonable facilities were not afforded to the public, such as they were entitled to demand, and that undue and unreasonable preferences and advantages were given to other branch lines in the neighbourhood.

Mr Justice Creswell obviously did not approve of this case, and merely remarked (one can almost hear the acidity in his tone) that 'just because a person could travel to Epsom or Wimbledon at a cheaper rate it did not show that any advantage was given to these places, but had there been a rival Company to the Caterham, it might have been different; and as to the complaint that trains did not stop at the junction, well, a railway company could not stop at every station merely to set down a passenger or two – on such a question the railway would be governed by the traffic'. Not even when trains were *booked* to stop? It would not be unjust to assume that Mr Justice Creswell may have had an interest of some description in the major companies. He unbent sufficiently when dealing with the question of accommodation at the junction, to rule that the Brighton Company must provide shelter there 'as it appeared that there were elsewhere on the line stopping stations' – whatever connexion that may have had in the matter. If he had added that it was disgusting that the common people should be provided with shelter at all, it would not have been out of keeping with his attitude. The well-to-do would have had their own carriages, and it is hard to believe that they would have patronised this small length of line when there was so much inconvenience to put up with.

As a last effort, Sir Fitzroy Kelly asked: 'Does not your Lordship think we are entitled to a rule for a refusal to grant third-class return tickets?' To which his Lordship succinctly replied: 'No, I think not.'

So far, not so good.

Herapath's Journal commented on the decision as 'appearing to be quite just'. It considered that if the Railway Regulation Act required equal fares per mile to be charged all over a line no matter how much circumstances differed, it would result in the greatest harm both to the public and the Companies. It was reasonable, too, it added, for the train service to be in proportion to the extent of the traffic.

Disheartened, the Caterham Company offered to dispose of the line to the Brighton or South-Eastern or both, but the main line companies, eyeing each other and the 1848 Agreement with distrust, were both nervous of making a direct move, and declined to accept any such proposal.

For about three or four months after this contest there was, superficially, peace and quiet, and it does seem as if, though legally defeated, Caterham was getting better conditions; even the South-Eastern provided trains which connected properly. This Company kept an open, if somewhat jaundiced, eye on the Brighton, which would, no doubt, try to squeeze the Caterham, buy it out and do it down; and then set off boldly into South-Eastern territory – and damn the Agreements! If any doing down was to be done, the South-Eastern preferred to use its own more practised hand.

There was, however, the small question of payment to the Brighton for hire of the engine, carriages and trucks. The terms of payment originally suggested by the Brighton were: engines and passenger carriages, 15 per cent. upon the actual value, the Caterham Company paying for all repairs thereto; stone wagons and coal trucks, one-eighth penny per mile run by each vehicle, empty trucks running at the same rate. After some haggling, the Caterham agreed to this, but failed to pay up for any vehicle hired. On 19 March 1857 the Brighton made some attempt to extract payment before 1 April, by threatening to withdraw the plant on that date. Caterham continued placidly to work its inadequate traffic, but failed to make any payment. The Brighton extended its withdrawal date to 1 May, provided payment was made by 15 April. To this, for the first time, Caterham made some sort of reply on the matter: they calmly said that 'the matter would be submitted to the Caterham Railway Board on *17 May*'! This snubbing attitude was apparently regretted a few days later, and the Caterham Chairman, Fuller, wrote that part-payment would be sent on or before 6 May. The Brighton demanded the Caterham Directors' personal guarantee, to which Fuller replied, with some spirit, that he declined to do any such thing. Tired of this unremunerative white elephant, and irritated by its placid indifference to its debts (the Brighton at that time thought money more important than anything else in the world) they approached the South-Eastern with a view to

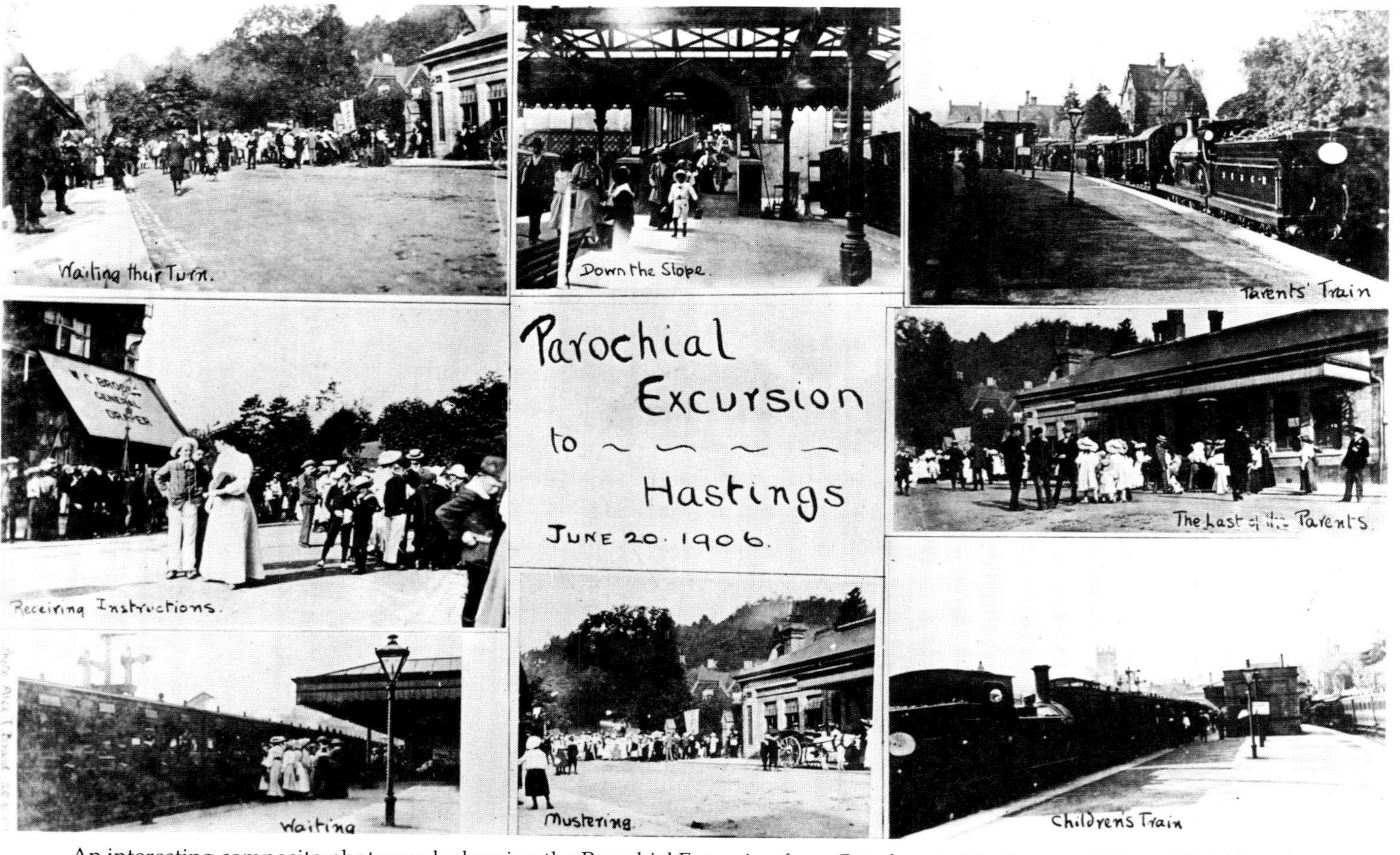

An interesting composite photograph showing the Parochial Excursion from Caterham to Hastings on 20 June 1906. Note the special for parents and another for children!

With station staff and engine crew posing beside a Cudworth locomotive for the camera, this photograph was taken in 1885 at Caterham. Did the South-Eastern always handle goods as the hamper on the platform suggests? And why 'COWDUNG' (*upside down*)?

Driver Cheney with his fireman and locomotive 'H' Class 0–4–4T No. 16 at Caterham in 1915 accompanied by wartime women carriage cleaners.

Late Hemming Collection

inserting advertisements in the newspapers on 1 May that both Companies would cease to book passengers to the Caterham line on and after 7 May.

On the day the advertisement appeared[1] the Brighton, having started the fuss, was secretly rather annoyed to receive a cheque from Fuller for £250, with a promise of the remainder by the end of the month, with a tart postscript that the money *would* have been paid by 6 May 'if the charge for coke had not been more than it should have been'. The line narrowly escaped being closed on 7 May, and a further £500 – certainly not the full amount owing – was sent on 29 May.

At the beginning of July, Caterham made a further attempt to get the Brighton to work the line. At the Brighton Board Meeting on 2 July, Leo Schuster, the Chairman, reported on this, and according to the Minutes, visited the South-Eastern offices and told them of the Caterham's proposal, saying the Brighton would decline to work the line. 'Mr. Schuster said that he had received communications from Gentlemen connected with the Caterham Railway Company, intimating that unless the Brighton and South-Eastern Companies were willing to work their line it will probably be shut up entirely in the course of next month. Mr. Schuster further intimated that from his own knowledge he could state that the Caterham Railway was at present being worked at a dead loss.'

There was no denying that the Caterham Railway was in desperate financial difficulties: traffic receipts for the first eleven months of working (i.e. up to 30 June 1857) were £854, and working expenses £1,700, a dead loss of £846, apart from the sundry debts.[2] The South-Eastern were asked by them if they would agree with the Brighton to make good some of the loss, by remitting to the Caterham Company a portion of the receipts from Caterham traffic on the main line. The only answer the South-Eastern would give was that they would be ready to consider any *definite* proposal, which was ineffectual, in that any proposal the Caterham made, if agreed to by the South-Eastern, would have been stamped on by the Brighton as infringing one of the various Agreements.

[1]Only the SE advertisement is to be found. Having got the SE to do the job, the Brighton presumably decided to save on their own advertisement.

[2]SER Minutes, 10 December 1857.

Chapter Six

The Main Battle

On 18 March 1857, there was written a Minute of the Joint South-Eastern and Brighton Committee, in which Leo Schuster, the Brighton Chairman, 'informed the Committee that he had received an offer from the Caterham Company to sell their line, under certain conditions, for £23,700, and he read such proposition to the Committee, and stated that he thought it inadvisable to leave such a line in the hands of an independent company, who might use it to the prejudice of the interest of the parent line; at the same time, the present offer was not such a one as he was prepared to listen to, although he might consent to a purchase at a more moderate sum.'

One point needs clarifying in that Minute; it was revealed later that Schuster had offered £16,000 to the Caterham, but no mention was made of this in the Minute. Did Schuster hoodwink the South-Eastern section of the Committee, by telling them, in a casual way, that an offer for sale had been received, without revealing all the facts? It must be remembered that the Committee concerned was a *Joint* Committee, and that South-Eastern members were in attendance, though they may have been old and difficult, and quite unable to understand what it was all about.

One might also question Schuster's statement that an independent company, left to itself, might use its line to the prejudice of the parent line. And what did he think the 4½ mile Caterham Company might do, mortgaged up to the hilt as it was? Bring out some grandiose scheme like the 'Manchester and Milford', and build a competitive line from London to Brighton? All the Caterham people wanted was fair treatment from either the Brighton or the South-Eastern, or both, but they got nothing.

The South-Eastern heard about the offer of £16,000 – probably from the mutual Director, Beattie, and the Secretary wrote to the Brighton as follows:

> 'I yesterday submitted to my Directors the draft Minutes of the Joint Committee meeting held on the 18th ult., which you were kind enough to forward to me on the 27th. Those Directors of this Company who were present on the occasion take objection to the record in as far as it respects what occurred with reference to the negotiation by Mr. Schuster for the purchase or lease of the Caterham Line, and the Board desire me to express to you their opinion that according to the spirit of the Agreement of July 1848, the district penetrated by the Caterham Railway is, and always has been, regarded as the South-Eastern District, and they therefore consider that any negotiation for the purchase or lease of the Line should rest with the South-Eastern Company.'

Then what, may one ask, were the South-Eastern people doing at

An early view of Caterham Junction (now Purley) in about 1880, with the tall signal-box on the platform.

With 1898 over the doors, the running shed at Purley was where the locomotives used on the branch were generally stabled. In 1926, when this photograph was taken, there was a good variety of company and private owners' wagons to be seen. *H.C. Casserley*

the meeting? Did they raise no objection at the time, or were they really asleep?

Within a few days the Brighton replied, and opened up by dismissing the 1848 Agreement with a perfunctory wave of the hand. It then went over the ground all over again: rubbing in about the inconvenience of an independent railway, explaining that the suggestion had been made to the South-Eastern Directors at the Joint Meeting that the difficulty should be removed by purchase or lease; and that Schuster had been attempting to carry out the negotiations with South-Eastern Directors' approval.

Argue, argue, argue! Oh, yes, and as a tailpiece: the sum of £16,000 *had* been offered for the purchase of the line, but had been declined by the Caterham Company. (Naturally – it had cost them nearly £40,000, partly through the Brighton's lack of generosity in demanding a new bridge over the Godstone-road, though such doubtful points were not, of course, mentioned to the South-Eastern.)

The South-Eastern promptly sent over two of their Directors, Mellor and Teulon, to an interview at the Brighton's fortress at the adjoining station at London Bridge, a somewhat futile performance in which they appear to have done nothing except sit and glare at each other, while the Brighton stated frankly, loudly, and several times, that the South-Eastern had 'misinterpreted' their letters.

For some time after this there was a deadlock; neither side could think of any new rude things to say. Further correspondence indicates that the South-Eastern went on harping on the 1848 Agreement (with occasional spasmodic references to that of 1854) while the Brighton calmly but firmly continued on the line that there were no 'negotiations', but only a *suggestion* of purchasing the Caterham, and that it was a Committee matter, and not a personal Brighton move. Having taken this stand, it was prepared to stick to it.

In fairness to the Brighton, one feels there is a ring of truth about its statements – or some of them – and the fact probably can be accepted that the South-Eastern Directors were perfectly well aware of what Schuster was saying, but simply did not pay attention. The only excuse that can be granted them for such conduct is that committee meetings of any description can be not only confusing but boring.

On 11 May, the Brighton wrote that a suggestion had been made to Messrs Mellor and Teulon that the solicitors of both Companies should look into the matter of the 1848 Agreement, and report thereon to the two Boards. 'My Directors,' continued Mr Slight, the Secretary, 'desire me to . . . add that their views of the Agreement, and of the understanding between the two Companies, remains unaltered, and that they are as anxious as the South-Eastern Company can be to act fully up to both its letter and its spirit, but as the two Companies

A sixteen coach combined Caterham and Tadworth train, climbing Brockley bank, hauled by a 4–4–0 tank engine No. 162.

Caterham station in 1932, with station-master Baker in attendance. The old station platform is seen on the right.

appear to differ somewhat in the reading of the particular clauses, it is in their opinion desirable that their actual bearing should be ascertained, and any possible difference removed.'

This was very sticky ground; especially in view of the fact that the Brighton knew, and the South-Eastern knew that they knew, that according to the 1848 Agreement, Caterham lay on the South-Eastern's side of the fence. The trouble lay in the fact that the junction with the Caterham was on the Brighton's portion of the Redhill–Croydon section. If a Caterham line had had its junction at a point south of Stoat's Nest, the Brighton would not have been in a position to argue. The South-Eastern in its reply, carefully pointed this out, and 'felt constrained to say that any attempt on the part of the Brighton Company to possess itself of the Caterham Railway without the written consent of the South-Eastern Company, would . . . be a breach of the existing covenants.' It is not easy to visualise the South-Eastern giving such written consent. The Directors added that they hoped they would receive an assurance that the Brighton would abstain from proceeding further in the matter.

It is here that the Brighton Directors made an error. They wrote on 8 June, avoiding altogether the issue of Agreements, but threatening that if the South-Eastern acquired possession of the Caterham, it would place itself in the same position as the Caterham – that is, have to pay toll to the Brighton.

One can imagine the stormy reception this letter got from the South-Eastern Directors, whose reply was prompt, and possessed an unusual element of truth in it; they also indulged in some sarcasm. In an interim letter, the Secretary said that he would submit the matter to his Directors, but:

> 'writes at present merely to correct an error into which you have inadvertently fallen . . . You have doubtless overlooked the circumstances that an Agreement exists between the two Companies, by which this Company possesses the right (not enjoyed by the Caterham Company) of running traffic toll free over that portion of your Railway which extends from the Croydon Railway to the junction with our main line near Stoat's Nest. Your remarks, therefore, I apprehend, can only apply to the Croydon Railway – the right of this Company to the free use of the line south of Croydon not having been disturbed in any respect by the Agreement of 1848.'

There is no trace of any reply – not even an acknowledgement – to this letter, the Brighton probably having become aware that it had overstepped the mark. However, any excuse was better than none, for had not even the South-Eastern referred to the *Croydon* Railway, which had been amalgamated with the Brighton eleven years earlier?

Correspondence was reopened in the following Autumn, the

South-Eastern Directors having by this time thought up a fresh line of attack. In their letter of 29 October 1857, they said that they had no intention or desire to purchase the branch, as they did not expect to derive any advantages from its possession. It ran:

> 'They [the Directors] are ready to admit that so long as the Caterham Company is in difficulties, its line holds out a temptation to the Mid-Kent Company[1] on one side, and to new lines extending eastward from the South-Western Railway on the other, to extend themselves towards it through Croydon, and thereby disturb the amicable arrangements existing between us. They are willing . . . to put an end to this state of things, in order that these amicable relations may be preserved . . .'

Here they started treading on dangerous ground again.

> 'Were the Caterham line extended to any point of our main line, you are aware that we should have the right of running our traffic by that route without being subject to Croydon toll . . . but they do not think it unreasonable . . . that you should treat the Caterham traffic as if such connexion had actually been formed.'

The Directors also suggested that the Brighton had pressed them into attempting to buy the line, but one feels they would have preferred to use the word *goaded*. They admitted that they were considering offering £16,000 for it, and that, in the circumstances, the Brighton should agree to their working the traffic to and from the district free of toll, subject to 'reasonable restrictions', agreed upon so that it would not interfere with the Brighton's local traffic. The sole object in purchasing the Caterham, they reiterated, was to prevent 'intrusion' from other companies.

On the face of it a not unreasonable letter, yet it required some skill in this war of nerves to make such a bold suggestion that the Brighton should consider a connexion from Caterham to the South-Eastern main line (presumably at or near Godstone) as already formed. The fact that they were permitted, according to the original arrangement, to run free of toll between Stoat's Nest and Croydon did not necessarily imply that they could do so by any other route.

The question of the Croydon toll is very confusing. By the 1848 Agreement, the South-Eastern had been excused this, although it referred, at that time, only to main line traffic from Redhill; presumably traffic from Caterham, even if eventually owned by the South-Eastern, was not to be granted this privilege.

The idea that the Mid-Kent might buy the Caterham, build a connexion between it and Beckenham, and extend southwards, was, of course, a possibility, though a faint one; but that the South-Western, which was not particularly interfering, should be dragged on to the scene, merely shows up the ludicrousness of the situation. The South-

[1]Opened from Lewisham to Beckenham, 1 January 1857.

Western certainly had an interest in the Wimbledon & Croydon line; they *might* have liked to buy the Caterham as a stepping-stone to South-Eastern territory. More likely the South-Eastern was guiltily thinking of its own particular effort in acquiring the Reading, Guildford and Reigate Railway, which brought it into Great Western territory at Reading, forty-six miles from its main stem.

This last letter of the South-Eastern was rather a hard nut for the Brighton Directors to crack, but they did their best and, after some weeks' thought, by blaming the Caterham Railway for all the trouble. The latter was accused, firstly, of not having produced some tangible proposition' – i.e. accepted the low price of purchase suitable to the Brighton's mentality, if not its pocket; and, secondly, of having failed to pay up for hire of plant, mileage share of traffic, etc. Consequently, the Brighton now gave a final notice to the Caterham that plant would be withdrawn as from 1 January 1858.

> 'I have been desired to forward you this early information thereof in order that no inconvenience may arise as regards the preparation of your January time-tables,'

was how the Brighton wrote to the South-Eastern. This kindly thought could not have impressed the South-Eastern very much, as it did not, in any case, include the Caterham Railway in its time-tables until shortly before it finally acquired the line. The Brighton ended with a final warning about

> 'preserving amicable relations, and, on that very account, must object to make any alteration in the toll payable . . . on traffic arising from such a line as the Caterham Railway.'

Caterham also informed the South-Eastern about the Brighton's latest threatened withdrawal of plant. The South-Eastern General Manager recommended to his Board that they should work the Caterham line on the following conditions:

1. South-Eastern to supply the Caterham with engines and carriages on the same terms as now supplied by the Brighton.
2. Receipts to include all traffic between the Caterham Railway and London, and its own local traffic.
3. £150 a month to be allowed the Caterham Company from the gross traffic of the Brighton and South-Eastern for working expenses; the remainder to be divided between the Brighton and South-Eastern.
4. The amount required for supply of plant by South-Eastern to be deducted from the Caterham's £150 allowance.
5. Receipts at Caterham, Warlingham and Kenley to be paid over daily to the South-Eastern.
6. Arrangements for working to continue in force until 31 July 1858, the South-Eastern to be at liberty to remove the plant earlier on giving a month's notice.

London, Brighton and South Coast Railway.

NOTICE.

On and after the 1st October next

THE NAME OF

CATERHAM JUNCTION

STATION

WILL BE

ALTERED TO

PURLEY.

(By Order) A. SARLE, Secretary & General Manager.

JULY 2nd, 1888.

The notice depicting the final change of name to Purley station dated 1888.

Right The extra train can only have run between East Croydon and Caterham Junction. The Caterham train left the Junction at 12.25, unless, of course, they

London, Brighton, & South-Coast Railway.

AN

EXTRA TRAIN

(1st and 2nd Class)

Will Run Daily (Sundays excepted)

BETWEEN

LONDON

AND

Caterham Junction,

COMMENCING

MONDAY, June 14th,

AS UNDER

DOWN.

Leave Pimlico (West-end) Terminus	-	11.45 a.m.
„ London Bridge - - -	-	12. 0 noon.
Arrive at Caterham Junction	(about)	12.31 p.m.

UP.

Leave Caterham Junction - -	-	12.40 p.m.
Arrive at London Bridge -	(about)	1.20 „
„ Pimlico - - -	„	1.25 „

Passengers between LONDON and CATERHAM Junction by the above Trains CHANGE CARRIAGES at CROYDON.

GEO. HAWKINS,
TRAFFIC MANAGER.

Terminus, Brighton, 5th June, 1880.

These conditions were merciless, for Caterham could hardly have hoped to earn more than a few pounds a month if they paid back, as they no doubt would have had to do, most of the £150 paid to them for 'working expenses'.

The Brighton was notified of this arrangement and, although no decision of theirs is to be traced, it seems that some agreement came into force whereby the South-Eastern *and* the Brighton shared the responsibility of providing the plant. It is not exactly clear what the Agreement was all about, but then the Brighton and South-Eastern were probably not very clear either.

In February 1858, the Secretary of the Caterham Company wrote to the South-Eastern about the valuation of the plant supplied. Engine and tender and first-, second- and third-class carriages were valued at £2,100.

In the meantime, the Brighton instructed their solicitors to bring an action against the Caterham Railway for the balance due for the hire of their plant from 1856–7.

Even during this period of financial turmoil, Caterham had no intention of sitting back and doing nothing. In March, Mr Juland Danvers demanded satisfaction regarding season tickets between London and Caterham, but the Brighton refused to issue anything except between London and the Junction. In May, Drew complained to the Brighton that the 4.10 pm down no longer stopped at the Junction, to which the Brighton replied that it had been discontinued 'from reasons of public safety, and in consequence of frequent complaints from the South-Eastern whose 4.25 express was brought into too close contact with the 4.10'. What they did not say was that the South-Eastern complained because the 4.10 pm was, more often than not, late. Operating conditions on the Brighton at this period were by no means good.

Then fell the final blow. In July 1858 appeared a notice in *Herapath's Journal* concerning Caterham, which ran:

'Ye who would speculate in new railways in this neighbourhood, read the following in yesterday's *Times*:–

"ROLLS COURT, Chancery Lane, July 22nd.
(*Before the* MASTER *of the* ROLLS)

FURNESS *v*. THE CATERHAM RAILWAY COMPANY.

The Plaintiff, as one of the contractors for the Caterham Railway, holds certain debentures of the Company, upon which about £3,000 remains unsatisfied. In April, 1857, the Plaintiff recovered judgment against the Company for the amount, and under a writ of *fieri facias*, an attachment has realised in the goods, chattels, and assets of the Company, about £120.

The Plaintiff subsequently obtained a writ of *elegit* against the Company's land, and by virtue of such writ, has been put in possession of the Railway and the Tolls of the same. These Tolls not being sufficient to satisfy the Plaintiff he now prays that the lands of the Company may be sold under the direction of the Court, and the proceeds appropriated in payment of himself and other incumbrances on the railway."'

The Judge appointed George Furness the Plaintiff receiver without salary, and, as creditor in possession of the line, he offered it to the South-Eastern for £16,000. The South-Eastern, having a different financial mentality, suggested £12,000. The line could not be bought without an Act of Parliament, but the Caterham Company realised that the end was in sight – they could not possibly continue to function as an independent concern – and at the request of the South-Eastern applied through the Contractor in November for power to lease or sell to that Company; *and* to repeal or amend any Acts which would prevent the South-Eastern from buying it – in plain English, do away with all the frivolous Acts which so far no one had taken very seriously.

On the 11th of this month, at a meeting of the Joint Brighton & South-Eastern Committee, the question of the South-Eastern's proposed purchase was tabled on the agenda, but the South-Eastern's Minutes report, rather curiously, that 'The South-Eastern members of the Joint committee withdrew to an adjoining room with the Deputation from the Brighton Company, on the subject of the purchase of the Caterham Railway, and on their return intimated that the projected line between Uckfield and Tunbridge Wells had been brought under notice, when the Brighton Directors stated their intention of opposing it'! The Brighton, it appears, were more concerned with Uckfield and Tunbridge Wells, and temporarily passed over the Caterham question as of secondary importance. The matter was not, however, entirely forgotten, for on the last day of 1858, the Brighton sent a New Year's greeting to the South-Eastern in the shape of a courteously-worded threat that it must withdraw from the use of Caterham Junction.

'The temporary arrangement made in December 1857 expired on 31st October last, and my Board did not desire to place any impediment in the way of your Company completing its Agreement with the Caterham Company, concurrently with which certain arrangements with this Company – as regards the stopping of your trains at the Caterham Junction, and the booking and carrying of passengers between East Croydon and stations on the Caterham line – would have been necessary. No such arrangement having been concluded, my Directors cannot, with due regard to preserving the rights of this

Company, allow matters to continue in their present position, and unless some arrangements are immediately concluded, they must withdraw their temporary permission by which your trains have been permitted to stop at the Caterham Junction . . .'

The South-Eastern quite rightly took the attitude that traffic was being worked under an Agreement of 29 November 1855, which had included 'all traffic between London and the junction with the Caterham Railway'.

This was not good enough for the Brighton Directors, who had suddenly woken up again. They maintained that the Agreement of 1855 had nothing to do with the case, as the Caterham line was not then open, and that it was not until just before that event took place – in the following July – that any agreement was made to permit the South-Eastern trains to stop at Caterham Junction. This was sheer quibbling: the letter went rambling on and on, repeating verbose legal phrases, and getting more and more confused. They dragged red herrings across everything, even to the extent of questioning the right of South-Eastern trains to stop at Forest Hill, which had nothing to do with the matter. They did not, they added, refer to the right of the South-Eastern to *run* trains to and from the Caterham line, but to the *stopping* of the trains at the Junction. The South-Eastern could do what it liked, provided the trains ran from Kenley to London Bridge non-stop, which was palpably absurd. But the South-Eastern was not to be put off; it merely refrained from answering. By this time it had taken over the working of the branch, operationally, if not legally. In April and May 1859, the train service was reduced from five to two trains each way daily, and all connexions at the Junction made by the South-Eastern only, the normal service being restored in June. The reduction was presumably due to operational difficulties.

In April 1859, the South-Eastern Law Clerk reported the results of proceedings in the House of Commons, referring to the Caterham Railway (*Sale Bill*) pending in Parliament. The Bill had passed Committee, with a clause added that South-Eastern trains should stop at Caterham Junction for Caterham line traffic only. The Brighton was expected to oppose the clause in the Lords, and the Law Clerk suggested writing to that Company, with a view to arranging a clause for the approval of both parties.

What happened next is not known. The remaining correspondence is with the Brighton Company's solicitors, with vague requests for 'a clause to be inserted which would meet with approval'. That such approval was eventually met with is fairly obvious, for on 7 July following, the Deputy-Chairman of the South-Eastern, William Gordon Thomson, had an interview with Leo Schuster, the Brighton

Chairman. It was agreed that the Brighton would now permit the South-Eastern to stop at Caterham Junction, to take up and put down Caterham traffic, for ten years, renewable.

No further trouble was reported with this Agreement, and in 1869–70 the London, Brighton & South Coast and South-Eastern agreed to pool and divide receipts between London and certain stations common to both companies, of which Caterham Junction, though physically a Brighton station, was one. Within ten years, too, both companies had forgotten the long drawn-out war over the unhappy Caterham Railway, and had found fresh fields on which to fight their pitched battles.

CATERHAM RAILWAY.

GOODS DEPARTMENT.

PUBLIC NOTICE.

The Caterham Railway Company (in connection with the London Brighton and South Coast Railway Company,) convey Goods at the following Rates per Ton, and subject to the undermentioned conditions :—

BRICKLAYERS' ARMS STATION, Willow Walk, Bermondsey,

	Special Class. s. d.	1st Class. s. d.	2nd Class. s. d.	3rd Class. s. d.	4th Class. s. d.	5th Class. s. d.
To Coulsdon / Warlingham / Caterham	2 8	3 1	3 6	5 0	6 11	7 11
CATERHAM to Warlingham, Coulsdon, or Godstone Road Junction	0 6	0 6	0 6	0 6	0 6	0 6
Croydon East / Forest Hill	2 8	2 11	3 1	4 10	6 2	7 7
Bricklayers' Arms	2 8	3 1	3 6	5 0	6 11	7 11

The Rates to and from the Thames Junction Wharf, Deptford, and the Commercial Docks, by the Branch Lines to these places, are the same as to and from Bricklayers Arms, but with an additional charge of 1s. 6d. per Ton for Wharfage, Porterage, &c., except on Special Class Goods, upon which the Wharfage at Deptford is 1s. per Ton.

THE CLASSES TO WHICH THESE RATES REFER ARE AS FOLLOW :—

Top section of large poster, mostly in very small print, of an original Caterham Railway notice regarding goods traffic, dated October 1856. The classes were, *Special*: Manure (all kinds except liquid), Bricks, Dung. *First*: Iron (old), Seaweed. *Second*: Ale, empty bottles, tallow. *Third*: Bacon, Bath bricks, Paper (coarse), Shumac (whatever that is). *Fourth*: Candles, Fancy Woods, Vegetables. *fifth*: Bedding, Feathers, poultry (dead).

Chapter Seven

Early Days under the South-Eastern

Thus the final chapter of the Caterham Railway's struggling independence drew quietly to a close with the transfer to the South-Eastern Railway, by an Act of 21 July 1859.[1] The undertaking, which had originally cost £39,367, was sold, lock, stock and barrel, for £14,000, with a further £1,200 to George Drew. This must have been a bitter blow to the promoters, but only the most optimistic could have hoped for any better results. With two powerful companies as neighbours, both of which started to wrangle over it even in its pre-natal days, it could not hope to make any headway. It was the fate of so many small independent lines of the period.

It is not always easy to assess reasons for failure, and in the case of the Caterham Railway, so much can be laid at the doors of the Brighton and South-Eastern Railways, solely on the score of petty bickering and mean behaviour. The promoters were not, of course, fully aware of the main companies' proclivities for abusing one another.

That traffic was, if not negligible, at any rate below the amount expected, is a fact that cannot be denied. The distance of the terminus from the Godstone Quarries was a factor very much against the success of the line; and as for passengers – one cannot squeeze blood out of a stone; the agricultural population of a rural area tends to stay put. What money was left from the little that came in was not even enough to pay for the various court battles.

From the point of view of the district, the sale was all to the good, if only because the South-Eastern would now have to foot the bills – and put up with poor receipts.

As it happened, the South-Eastern was lucky, for Drew's building programme at Caterham was beginning to bear fruit. It was due to his efforts that the path through the Harestone valley was made into a carriage-road, serving a number of large residences for the well-to-do. Incidentally, it is due in great measure to the owners of the houses that these valleys became the glory of trees and shrubs that they are today, for at that date the valleys around Caterham were comparatively treeless. Along the main road, too, buildings were appearing, made from the local stone, and Caterham Valley was slowly becoming a place. Nevertheless, it was not for nearly forty years that the South-Eastern paid much attention to local needs, except for occasional betterment of services and a slight reduction in fares.[2]

In January 1861 a slip coach service was put into operation at Caterham Junction, off the 1.30 pm South-Eastern train from London Bridge, which called at Croydon, Red Hill, Tunbridge,[3] Ashford, and

---

[1]22 and 23 Vic., cap. 35.

[2]Season ticket rates in 1863 were: first-class for three months (*see footnote on page* 30) £7 7*s.* 0*d.* from Caterham, Warlingham or Kenley; second-class £6 5*s.* 0*d.*

[3]Renamed Tonbridge in 1893 in conjunction with the Post Office, to avoid confusion with Tunbridge Wells.

stations to Dover. The slip portion was not, however, intended for Caterham, but formed a slow train to Red Hill, Reading and Maidstone lines. The word 'slip' not then being in use for this purpose, Bradshaw described it in a delightful way as 'Carriages detached: the Train does not stop' – an expression which must have made some passengers wonder.[1] Three months later, an extra slip was detached from the 4.20 pm express, fast to Tunbridge Wells. There was a connexion to Caterham off this train, but through running between London and Caterham does not appear to have been begun until about five years later.

By August of the same year, three slips were being made at the Junction, and these gradually grew in number until in 1865 there were six, with one extra on Mondays and Wednesdays. The number then gradually decreased until in 1875, there was only one operating, and this was finally withdrawn after January 1879, never to be revived.

In 1860, the Law Clerk, upon investigating the title of the Caterham Railway, discovered that in the Conveyance of Drew and a Captain Wigsell, there were contained Covenants on the part of the Caterham Railway – by which the South-Eastern as new owners would be bound – relating to the perpetual maintenance of a station at Kenley, and the stopping of a minimum number of passenger trains each way per day. After 'much negotiation' the Covenants were released, on Drew and Wigsell receiving an 'assurance' from the General Manager. Whether or not this assurance meant that the service at Kenley would be maintained, it is a fact that from February 1861 to August 1865, Kenley was reduced to the status of what, in later years, would have been called a 'halt'. It was officially described as a 'signal-stop' – that is, passengers wishing to be set down had to 'inform the Guard at the preceding *stopping* station'. As there was no express work on the branch, it is unlikely that there was much confusion.

Sunday trains on the branch were withdrawn between February 1862 and May 1865. This was probably an economy measure, though it is possible that local sabbatarians demanded their withdrawal.

The midnight train from Charing Cross first appeared in April 1867, and ran on Thursdays only. It was actually a Dorking train, but by changing at Caterham Junction, passengers could arrive at Caterham at 12.55 am. This became a regular daily train in 1881.

---

[1]Officialdom claims the first recorded slip coach to have been on the Brighton Railway at Hayward's Heath (for Hastings) in February 1858, and it is, in fact, reported in the *Railway Times* at that time. However, the South-Eastern's own company timetable for *January* 1858 (and possibly before) shows a slip off the 4.30 pm London–Hastings train via Ashford at *Godstone*. 'Leaves London passengers at Godstone, Paddock Wood and Staplehurst. The Train does not stop at Godstone or Paddock Wood.' The 4.25 pm from London to Hastings direct did a similar thing to a slip at Etchingham, but although the train left London earlier, the time of the Godstone slip would have been earlier than that at Etchingham. The purists can argue that one out!

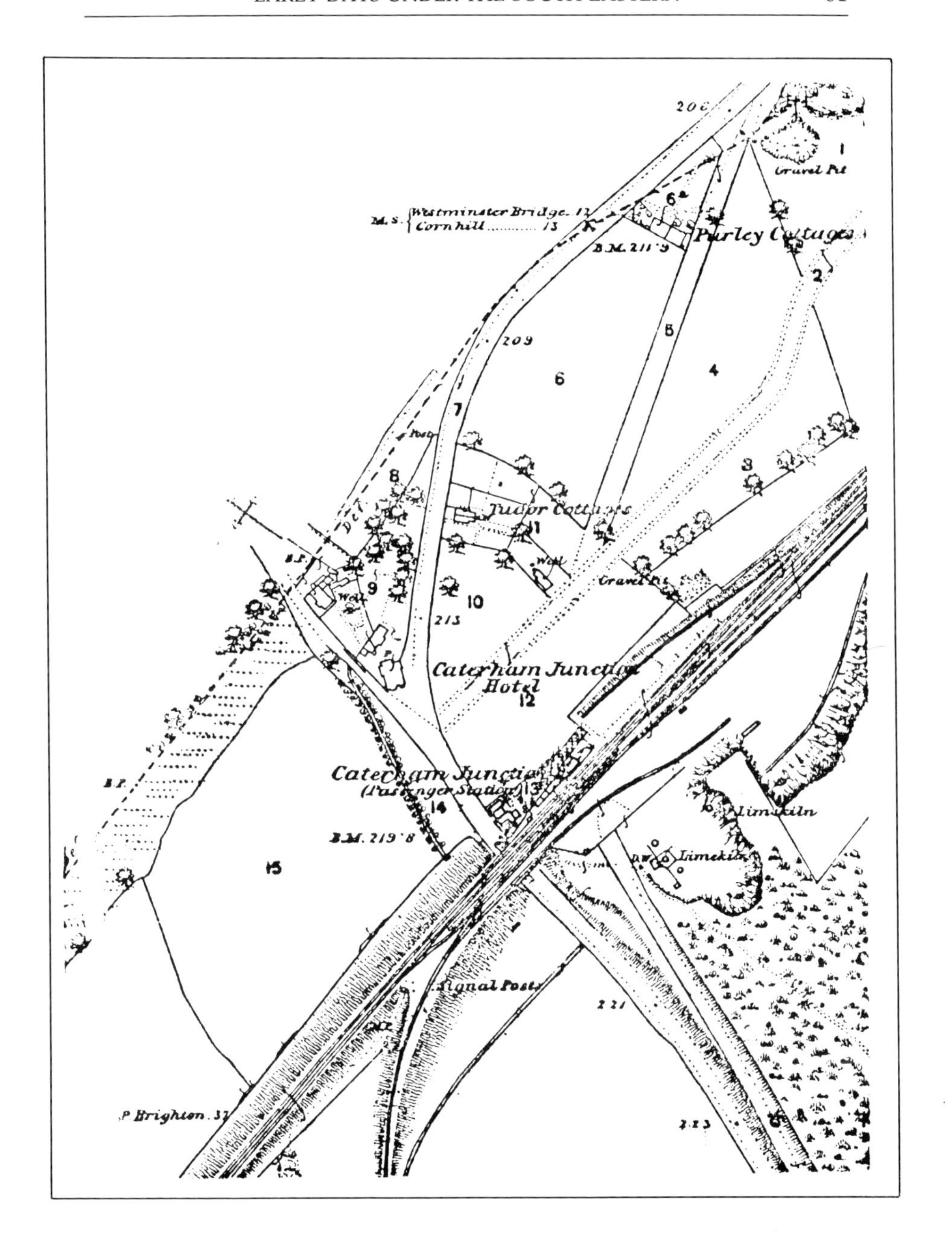

Plan of Caterham Junction in the 1860s, taken from an early Ordnance Survey map.

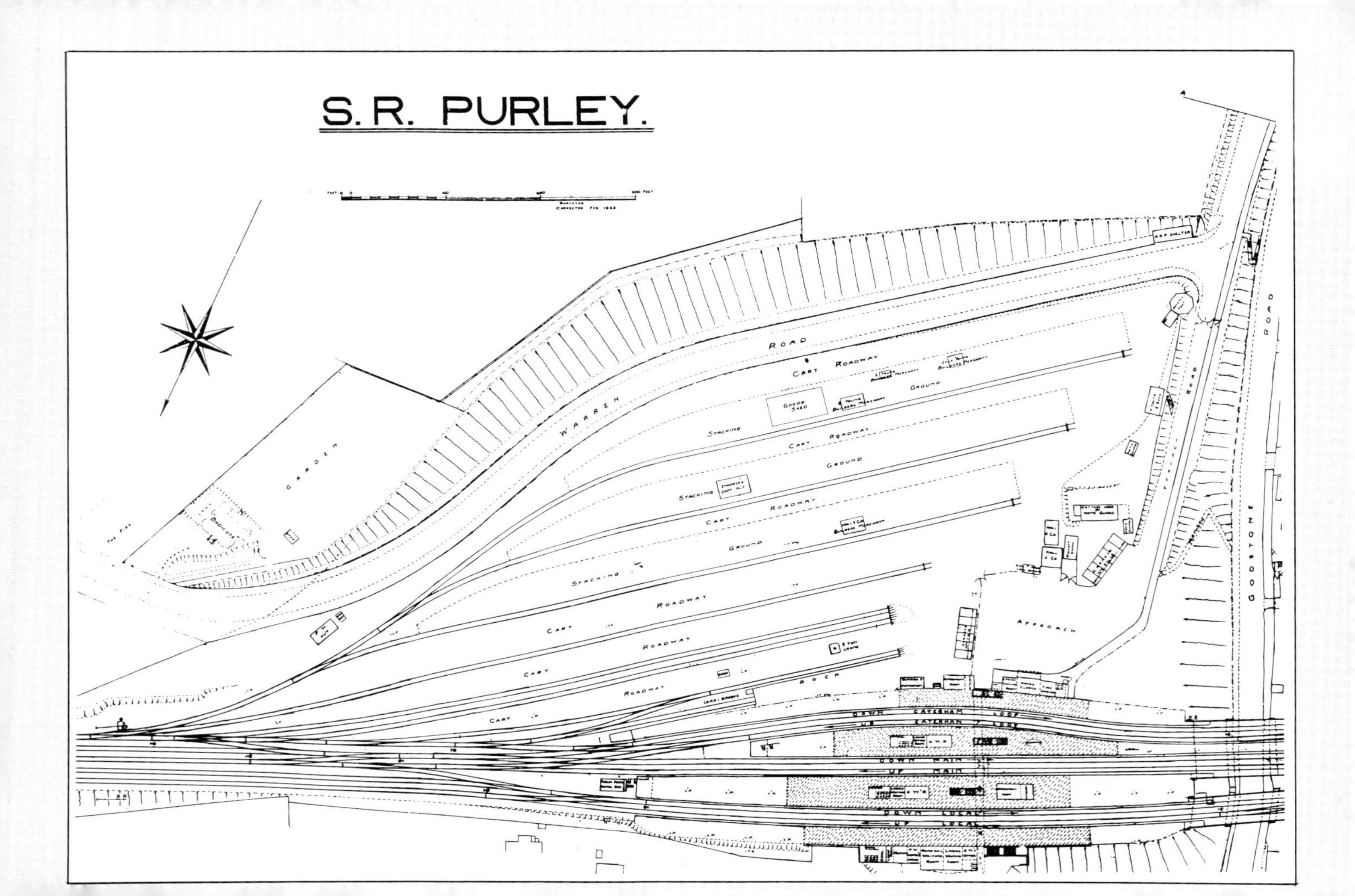

S.R. PURLEY.
WARREN ROAD
GODSTONE ROAD
CART ROADWAY
STACKING GROUND
GOODS SHED
GARDEN
APPROACH
DOCK
DOWN CATERHAM LOOP
UP CATERHAM LOOP
DOWN MAIN
UP MAIN
DOWN LOCAL
UP LOCAL
A.R.P. SHELTER

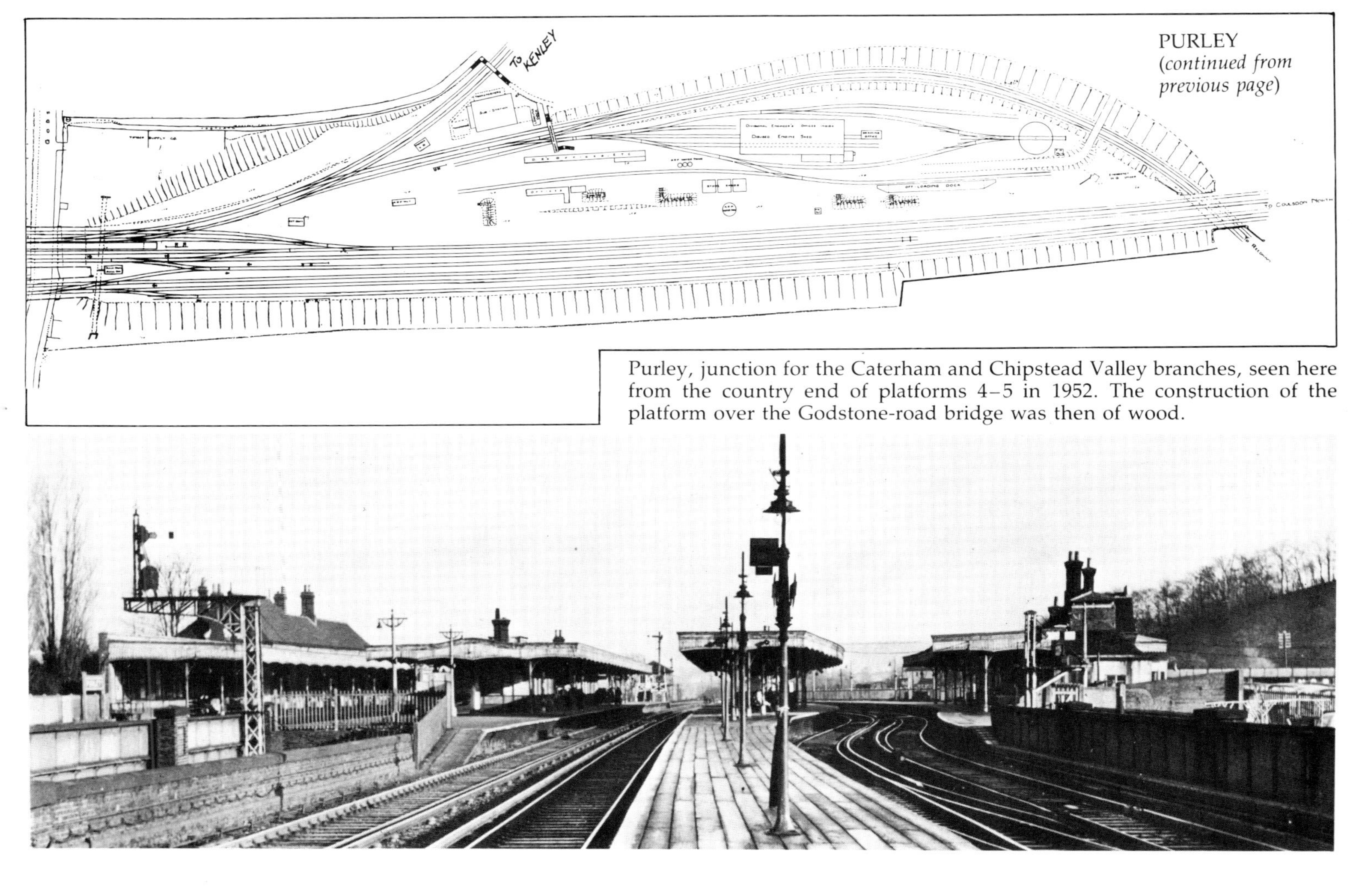

Purley, junction for the Caterham and Chipstead Valley branches, seen here from the country end of platforms 4–5 in 1952. The construction of the platform over the Godstone-road bridge was then of wood.

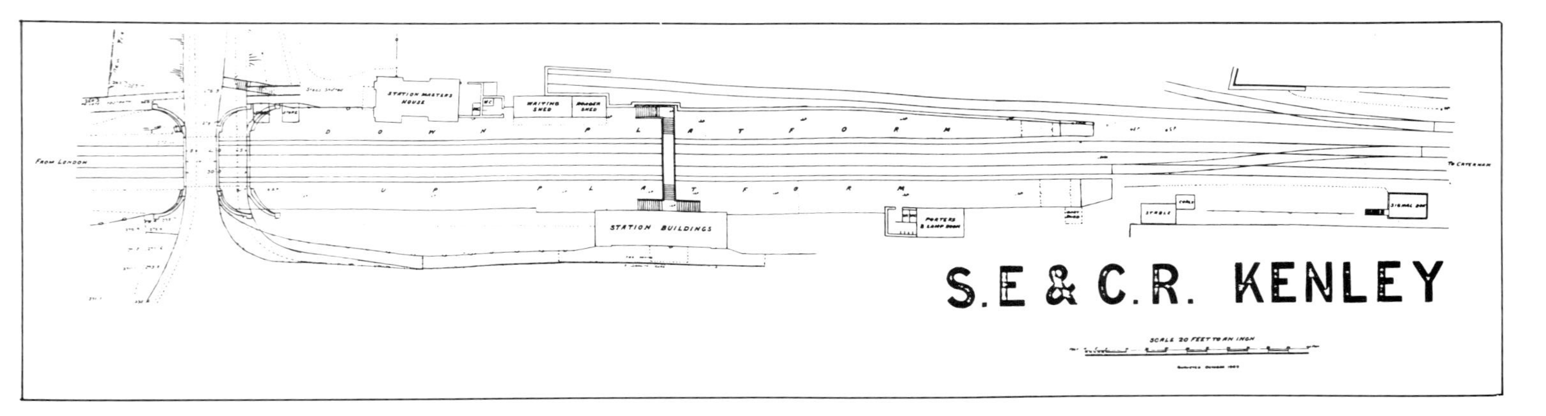

Kenley station taken from a coloured postcard in the 1930s.
Lens of Sutton

Old Postcard view of Kenley station. *Lens of Sutton*

Kenley station up side, possibly July 1899. *Lens of Sutton*

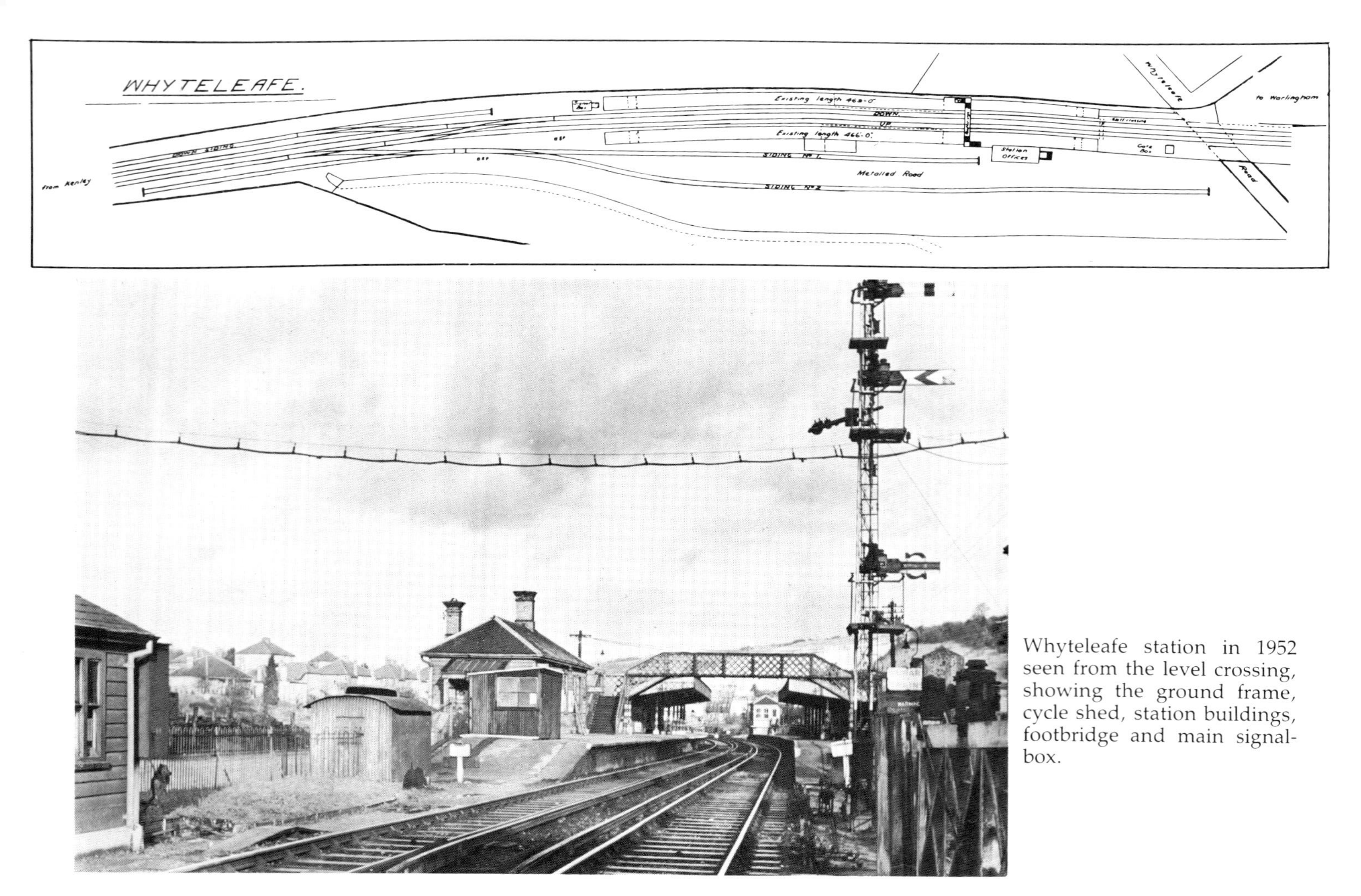

Whyteleafe station in 1952 seen from the level crossing, showing the ground frame, cycle shed, station buildings, footbridge and main signal-box.

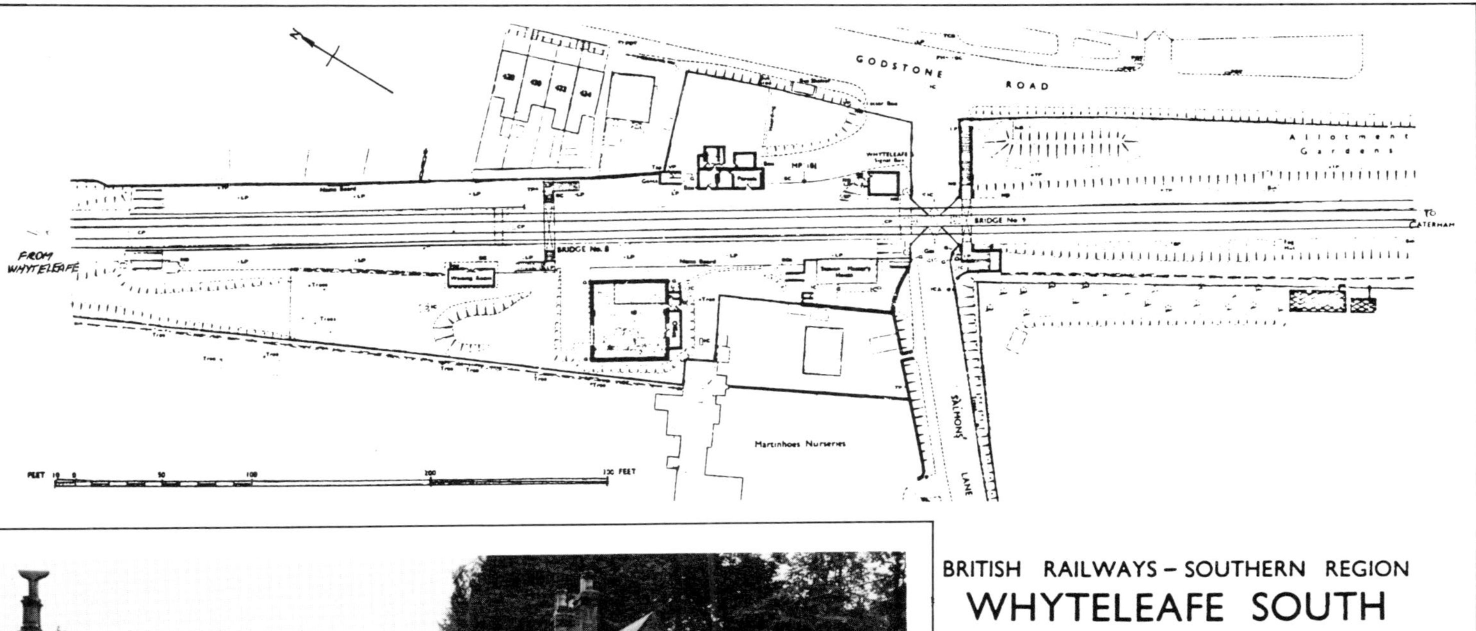

Whyteleafe South in the late 1950s.
Lens of Sutton

Top Warlingham, before June 1956 showing Purley to Caterham train, with headcode at wrong end, and
Bottom as Whyteleafe South, passengers waiting for a glimpse of the Caterham Centenarian. The footbridge under which the photographer was standing has long since been demolished. *Both photographs Lens of Sutton*

Ordinary fares, reduced slightly after the South-Eastern took over, were raised again in 1870. By 1884, return tickets available for four days were issued, the third-class fare from Caterham to London being 2*s*. 6*d*.

From January 1863, workmen were considered as being eligible for cheap travel, by the issue of third-class return tickets from Caterham and Warlingham to London on Saturdays, as Bradshaw says: 'to return by the 8½ mrn. train on Mondays'. The fare for the double journey was 1*s*. 6*d*. This was no doubt for the benefit of labourers imported to Caterham for the great housing operations which were spreading all over the district. Otherwise one would have thought that the week-end was the one time that workmen (or anyone else for that matter) would have preferred to remain at home.

The plum of this period, 1860 to 1870, was the great Caterham Railway grievances scandal, which produced a crop of pseudonymous letters in *The Times*, especially from those in Caterham itself who had been subjected for so long to the high-handed attitude of the two main companies. Gradually the storm of protest grew, and the name Caterham became a household word. *The Times*, which on the appearance of the first of these letters, had printed one and a half columns of a bitingly humorous Fourth Leader, realised that the situation was less amusing than it had at first appeared, and ended by printing such a damning attack on the Brighton and South-Eastern, that these two companies hurriedly convened a meeting 'with a view to improving the service and doing away with the cause of present complaints.'[1] Caterham was at last on the map.

In 1862 the Brighton and South-Eastern were indulging in one of their more violent 'hate' periods. These occurred from time to time, from 1842 to 1922, and sometimes led to the most alarming situations. In 1862, for no very obvious reason, the Brighton more or less forbade the South-Eastern the use of East Croydon, which was, of course, Brighton property. Passengers from Caterham (or for that matter, anywhere else on the South-Eastern) were not allowed to use the station unless they held a ticket issued by the Brighton Company. From Caterham, passengers for Croydon could book by South-Eastern to Caterham Junction, and there re-book on the Brighton, but that meant letting the South-Eastern train go and waiting several hours for the Brighton train (only four down and three up trains stopped there daily); or they could book by South-Eastern through to London, and re-book there to Croydon by the Brighton – a total distance of about 28 miles instead of eight!

The first letter appeared on 4 October, signed by 'Viator Vindex' of Lindfield, Sussex, and occupied half a column of close print. He was,

---

1 LB&SCR Minutes, 13 October 1862.

one suspects, a young man who, to a certain extent, enjoyed the ridiculous situation.

> 'I believe it is a matter of notoriety,' he wrote, 'that the Brighton and South-Eastern Companies, being unable to agree with each other, have long put the patient British public to the utmost possible inconvenience to gratify their private quarrels. Last week, having business in Caterham, I took the 9.5 train from Hayward's Heath which is advertised to stop at Caterham Junction, naturally concluding that a branch train would meet it. Arrived at the junction, I found that the branch train had been fixed to start three minutes before the arrival of our train, and there was no choice but to wait four hours or walk, no vehicle being to be had for love or money. I walked, and having transacted my business at Caterham, returned by the twelve o'clock train. I asked for a ticket to Hayward's Heath, but the clerk could only give me one as far as the junction, and there there was no down train for five hours. So I proposed to take the next up train and return by Croydon or London.
>
> "You must wait till 3 o'clock, Sir," said the porter.
>
> "What!" said I. "Are all these Caterham passengers kept here for five hours?"
>
> "Oh, no Sir, they are going on in twenty minutes, but you cannot go by that train as we are not allowed to book by it from this station, and they have through tickets from Caterham."
>
> I asked for a through ticket, and was refused one. I replied: "It ought to have been explained to me. What is to be done?"
>
> "Oh, there is no alternative, Sir, but to wait here five hours or walk."'

The bewildered man then said he would get into the train without a ticket, but the porter (and, apparently by now the stationmaster too) said they could not allow that, or they would be blamed for letting him get in. Having, as he put it 'freely expressed myself of their masters,' he attempted to get into the South-Eastern train bound for London, which had just drawn in. The stationmaster and porter, loyal Brighton employees that they were, tried to stop him.

> 'They seized me from behind, but their united efforts failed to move me, and my coat-tails, being fortunately stout, remained on my back, for which no thanks to my assailants, who were duly chaffed for their prowess by the men of Caterham.'

The stationmaster took his name and address, but apparently terrified of the consequences of his action in letting a would-be Brighton ticket-purchaser travel on a South-Eastern train, accompanied him to East Croydon, probably aghast at the idea that not only had his 'prisoner' no ticket of any description, but that he himself, as a Brighton employee, would be seen by his mates getting out of a train belonging to the unmentionable concern next door. Some railway Bible-puncher might even use it against him in chapel the following

Sunday. They were coldly received by the Brighton officials at Croydon, who refused to take the proffered fare. Meanwhile, the stationmaster fluttered about uneasily. Croydon said they would have three ways of treating his case, and that he would hear from them soon. He does not say how he returned eventually to Hayward's Heath, nor whether the stationmaster accompanied him back to Caterham Junction, but he ends his letter:

> 'After ten days nothing has been heard, but I think the public should have a chance to hear of it. I suggest . . . for the consideration of our Legislature next Session, whether a Bill should not be introduced to empower the President of the Board of Trade to intervene between railway companies and the public, upon representation being made to him, and substantiated to his satisfaction, that any two rival companies are wilfully putting the public to inconvenience of unnecessary delays at junction stations for the purpose of avenging their private quarrels.'

The Times pounced on this letter and started its Leader with a bang:

> 'The art of ingeniously tormenting, which in past days was considered exclusively a domestic study, is now cultivated with eminent success by the managing authorities of British Railways . . .'

and followed this up by a long and humorous account of the unfortunate correspondent whom, incidentally, they accused of 'violating the law' by getting into the train without a ticket to effect 'a forcible and illicit escape from the clutches of his sworn torturers,' a remark which produced a further long letter from 'Viator Vindex'. The Leader ended, rather pointedly, with:

> 'We should not think that any Board would like to have the Caterham story told twice of a line under its control.'

Two days later appeared a letter from Caterham, signed by 'A Helot', who pointed out the absurdity of the situation by which they were not allowed to use East Croydon station.

> 'But this is not all,' continued the helot. 'If there were no railway at all, we should have carriers and omnibuses, but nobody will set up any conveyance for fear the [Railway] Directors that are quarrelling should come to their senses and run it off the road by allowing us to use the line as we used to do before the dispute broke out. Thus the railway will neither carry us itself nor let anyone else. What have we done to deserve such treatment? Pray, Sir, help us. We have no other hope. The railways have it all their own way in the House of Commons, and the Court of Common Pleas won't move, and if you can't put matters to rights and rescue us from this slavery, nobody else can.'

Another wrote that he was 'unable to reach a dying relative in time to see her alive' (in some ways the mid-Victorians were very uninhibited about death, especially when writing to newspapers), but that he received from the South-Eastern a polite and businesslike reply to his protest, but from the Brighton only a flippant one, 'showing very plainly where the bad feeling prevails.'

A man and his wife from Croydon, also visiting the sick of Caterham, were unable to buy Caterham tickets at East Croydon, so they travelled without, but the guard was a South-Eastern man, and raised no objection. Apparently half the Brighton staff at East Croydon tried to evict them but they refused to budge once they were in the train, and the guard stopped any further nonsense by blowing his whistle. At Caterham, these unlucky people had to pay the whole fare from London, and the writer commented: 'I think it is hardly just that the South-Eastern Company should thus make up the losses they suffer through the spiteful proceedings of their rivals.'

Some light relief in the correspondence soon came along.

> 'Towards the end of last season I sent my groom, with my horse, to meet me at the Croydon station. When at Croydon I missed my pocket-handkerchief, and, before I found it, and could pass some ladies' crinolines – no other passengers getting out – the train was in motion as I called with my head out of the door. This only created a laugh at seeing me in my hunting toggery thus carried away. At Caterham junction I got out, and a train came up at the moment. I rushed to a carriage, and was getting in when the stationmaster of the Brighton line pulled me back, saying that an addition to the fare that I had paid to Croydon was due to the South-Eastern line, and that, moreover, he was not allowed to let passengers get in by that train. I paid a trifling extra fare, and had to wait till the next Brighton train came up – in the meantime telegraphing to Croydon to detain my horse. Now, as perhaps some of your proprietors may be hunting men, they and others will be able to appreciate the annoyance to an
>
> OLD FOXHUNTER.'

There was also a letter from 'Barrister,' attempting to explain the difficulties, but in defence of whom it is not possible to tell, as it was written in legal terms, making it untranslatable into normal English.

Captain Bonus, commanding the 2nd Surrey Rifle Company, which had its range on Riddles Down, complained that they were unable to use the Kenley station, because of the Croydon ban, and instead of a 10-minute train journey (perhaps) had a four-mile march, often in pouring rain.

The Times, in its bitter attack in a Leader on 14 October, concluded with:

> 'As great movements often originate in particular grievances, it is not impossible that our Railway Companies may have cause to remember the day when an unfortunate passenger was tormented at Caterham junction.'

There was nothing even a railway company would not do if pressed hard enough, and it was only a few days before the question was reported as settled, and the South-Eastern allowed to set down and pick up their passengers at East Croydon.

In 1867, gas was laid on at Caterham Junction by the Croydon Gas Company, who charged 4*s*. 9*d*. a thousand for the gas, the cost of laying pipes and fittings (about £130) being borne by the Brighton. Kenley, Warlingham and Caterham were fitted with gas in 1873 at a cost of £73.

There were the usual complaints and 'memorials' from time to time. In July 1871 the South-Eastern were asked by Caterham residents 'to convey Ladies to London one day each week at reduced fares for marketing and shopping'. Like many other matters, the decision was deferred, and nothing more was heard.

In January 1873 the Chairman of the South-Eastern (Sir Edward Watkin) read, at a meeting of the Board, a complaint that there were no footwarmers on the Caterham line, and that Caterham Junction station was 'in a dirty state'.

That Caterham Junction was not entirely satisfactory from the point of view of accommodation is evident from the accident reports of 1873. On 22 September of that year, a Mr John Pickersgill-Cunliffe, in crossing the lines from the down to the up platform 'absorbed in a newspaper which he was perusing at the time,'[1] in order to catch a train leaving the Caterham Junction at 10.9 am for London, was struck by the footstep of the engine of a train from Brighton and knocked down; he died a fortnight later from injuries received. He lived in the Coulsdon district.

At the inquest it was said that between 300 and 400 people used the crossing daily. 'There would be little difficulty,' says the accident report, 'in carrying out improvements at this station, which are urgently required with a view to the safety of the public. The down platform should be widened, proper conveniences should be provided, and a subway should be formed under the main lines of the railway.'

Up to this date, and even until the subway was opened at the end of 1874, passengers were apparently permitted to wander about all over the lines in an effort to catch a train from the up platform. But it is small consolation to live on the South-Eastern Railway, and be killed by a Brighton Company's train on Brighton Company's property.

Joint South-Eastern and Brighton proposals were put forward for the alterations at the Junction, at an estimate of £2,000, but the Brighton plans were favoured by the Board of Trade, doubtless much

[1] *Croydon Chronicle*, 27 September 1873.

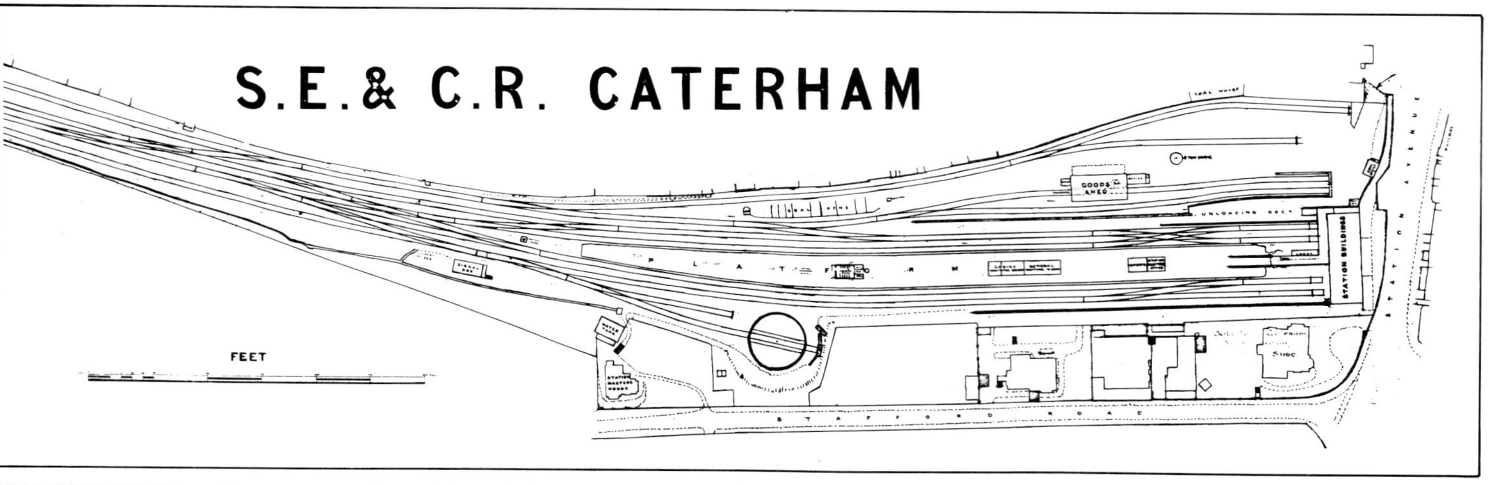

Caterham station, looking towards the buffers, before electrification was completed 1927. The goods yard and shed on left are now occupied by a supermarket.
Courtesy David & Charles, LGRP Collection

The scene outside Caterham station in 1952 with some fine old cars and vans to be seen. The coal office is now part of a supermarket, and the telephone boxes – concrete lined – have gone.

Caterham station in 1952, with Purley train at the platform, and the daily goods in the yard. The rather enormous building on the left was the cinema, long since gone. The Railway (Valley) Hotel is immediately in front of St John's Church, and a gaunt supermarket now obliterates them both.

to the mortification of the South-Eastern. Further alterations were made up to 1876, and the Brighton suggested that the South-Eastern should contribute. Indeed, so annoyed were the Brighton at their rival's aloofness, that when a South-Eastern engine was derailed there the following year, Mr Knight, General Manager of the Brighton, in reporting it at a Board Meeting, 'drew attention to the fact of great inconvenience constantly experienced at Caterham Junction, owing to the present mode of working the South-Eastern's Caterham traffic, for which over £6,000 had been paid in constructing a new station without drawing any pecuniary benefit therefrom.' It was suggested (by the Brighton) that the Caterham line should become joint property, and additional lines built from South Croydon to Caterham Junction. This provoked a lengthy and somewhat vituperative argument between Watkin and Laing (the Brighton Chairman), but they disagreed for so long that the subject was dropped.

The present station at Purley was opened in 1899, due in large measure to the construction of the new avoiding line from South Croydon to Stoat's Nest and Earlswood.

Applications for subscriptions for various charitable institutions were frequently received by railway companies. The South-Eastern were asked for a subscription for a proposed Parsonage House at St John's, Caterham, in 1874, and also towards building a School House at Caterham. Both were declined 'on the usual grounds' – whatever they were. In the case of the Voluntary Schools at Kenley, however, they contributed £100 when they discovered that the Brighton were doing to same. Jealousy can produce unexpected generosity even in railway companies.

An amusing incident occurred at the hundredth half-yearly meeting of the South-Eastern in July 1886, when an 85-year-old shareholder from Caterham, W.J. Gwynn, the builder, tried to move an amendment that the Directors should receive no emolument 'until they had done justice to Caterham'. The antagonistic Sir Edward Watkin was in the chair.

> CHAIRMAN: '. . . Now, gentlemen, I must tell you that my night's rest has been greatly disturbed by a note I have received from Mr. Gwynn of Caterham, about his moving an amendment to our Report. I must say that I think Mr. Gwynn is suffering rather from imaginary than from real grievances; but still I will say to Mr. Gwynn and to everybody who lives between London Bridge and Redhill that if we can succeed in inducing the Brighton to give up to us the legitimate and fair use of our own property between London Bridge and Redhill, we shall of course be able to run a larger number of trains . . . I do not think there is very much to grumble at.'

Here Watkin put on his most irritating manner.

'I see there are 25 trains each way between London and Caterham. I see that they all carry third-class passengers. I see that 82½ per cent. of the traffic is third-class. I see that the fares to Caterham are lower than to other places in the same district. I see that the train services have been much improved, passengers by the most convenient and best trains not having to change at Caterham Junction as formerly. When the Charing Cross line was opened the only increase in season tickets was £1 for first-class and 25*s*. for second-class; there was no addition when Cannon Street was opened . . . There is no substantial grievance at all. Everything possible has been done and will be done for the benefit of Caterham. We cannot satisfy every builder of houses in every district, gentlemen (*laughter*). The builders with a certain number of houses on their hands say it is the fault of those wretched railway people (*laughter*) forgetting that without the railway there would have been no houses at all. Mr. Gwynn . . . has been good enough to favour us with a small investment, made two or three years ago in the stock of the Company, I think £100 (*laughter*) . . . I do not know what it is he wants; what he asks now is that we should do something to reduce your dividend; I do not think that is a likely way to induce him to put Capital in the Company (*laughter*) . . .'

MR. GWYNN: 'I have complained, Sir, of your raising the fares . . . Here is the book to show it. I have laid out £20,000 at Caterham, and if encouraged, would lay out £20,000 more . . . We were prospering until you cruelly raised the fares. I wish you to go back to your old fares to Caterham, that it may prosper again. I move "That the Directors have no emolument until they do justice to Caterham." (*Laughter.*) . . . Some time ago, I applied for two trains; those trains were, after a time, put on, one out of Caterham somewhere about 11, another (*cries of "Time"*) something after 6. What was the consequence? The first train had not been on a fortnight before there was £30,000 worth of ground sold for building purposes. (*Interruptions and cries of "Can't hear", "Speak up".*) Gentlemen, you must make allowances for me; I am over 85 years of age. We went on prospering till you raised the first- and second-class fares, and now there are hundreds of houses to let at any price. Caterham is being ruined by these high fares. There is no healthier place than Caterham. Why not aid it?'

CHAIRMAN: 'Gentlemen, the amendment is "That the Directors shall not receive any pay till they do 'justice to Caterham'." (*Laughter.*) If I thought that would improve Caterham, which is suffering like all other places from bad times, I would do without pay for a long period. The amount taken between Caterham and London is £21 for a first-class annual ticket . . . roughly 15,000 miles in a first-class carriage for £21. Is that too much?'

MR. GWYNN: 'I am not complaining of the annual but of the single-ticket . . . I want you to return to the old fares . . .'

CHAIRMAN: 'People travel 40 miles for 2*s*. 6*d*. . . .'

MR. GWYNN: 'You are making a mistake, Sir, Here is the old table.'

The Chairman was somewhat taken aback by this proof of South-Eastern greed, and promised Mr Gwynn that the General Manager would look into the matter again. 'We could be of more service to Caterham and elsewhere if the Brighton Company did not crowd us out with an excessive number of trains,' he added, trying to cover the confusion by the instinctive method of blaming everything on the Brighton. Mr Gwynn, however, not to be put off, reminded him that it was the old fares he wanted, not more trains. One feels that if Mr Gwynn's age had not been against him, the battle might have gone on for some time, and Watkin did not like criticism.

Like 'Viator Vindex', our hero of 1862, Gwynn brought Caterham into the public eye again, and, despite Watkin's sneering attitude towards the older man, some attention was paid to the Caterham branch. It was better to give way a little than to have too many complaints.

Between 1863 and the early ' eighties, there came a spate of projected lines in the district, of which only two got further than discussion, taproom talk, and depositing of plans with the Clerk of the Peace for the County.

Plans were deposited by the South-Eastern in 1863 for a line from Woodside to Croydon (the present Addiscombe branch), and to the Caterham line, over the route from Woodside to Selsdon Road at that time under construction. It was to run through what is now the goods yard at Purley and join the Caterham branch a short distance from the Junction. This would conveniently have avoided using the Brighton line to Purley, but the Agreement made with that line in 1864 – similar to that of 1848 – put them once again on a more friendly footing in this area, at any rate temporarily, and the Caterham portion of the scheme was dropped.

By the Act of 6 July 1865, there was incorporated the Surrey & Sussex Junction Railway – the forerunner of the present Oxted line. It was a scheme which, though nominally independent, was backed by the Brighton, to connect up Croydon with its Tunbridge Wells and Uckfield line, and to continue from near Hailsham to Hastings. Owing to the new Agreement of 1864 it looked as if trouble was on the way, and it was. The South-Eastern was provoked into temporarily settling its differences – and there were many – with the London, Chatham & Dover Railway, and dragging that Company into projecting a line known as the London, Lewes & Brighton. This would have turned the tables on the London, Brighton & South Coast's attempt to compete for the Hastings traffic by competing for the Brighton traffic. The London, Lewes & Brighton never got beyond receiving its Act owing largely to the Chatham Company's withdrawal from the scheme, due either to lack of spirit, or money, or both. A considerable part of the Surrey & Sussex Junction was constructed, especially between Riddles Down and Groombridge, amongst the completed structures being the Woldingham Viaduct.[1] By 1869 the Brighton had lost nearly £500,000 in backing the scheme, and in that year powers were sought to transfer the line to that Company, which was ordered to complete the railway under a penalty of £50 a day. In 1870 the Brighton was refused permission to abandon the line, and it found itself in the unenviable position of having to complete a now unwanted line. It preferred to pay the daily penalty, which was limited to a total of £32,250, and the powers automatically lapsed.

The South Caterham Railway Bill was lodged in the Parliamentary Session of 1873. It was to leave the London, Brighton & South Coast Railway, as the circular so pedantically puts it, 'at a point on the siding which connects the main down line at the southern end of the Caterham Junction station, with the rails of the goods yard of the same station, and which point is 60 yards north-eastward of the semaphore signal, south-westward of the same station.' Could anything be clearer than that? It was to climb up a valley – mostly at a gradient of 1 in 53 – past Old Coulsdon, and end at a spot in Upper Caterham known as the Money Pit, 'in a field belonging to, or reputed to belong to, Thomas Grub.' There was also to be a loop at the Junction end, running through a deep cutting to join the original Caterham branch.

In the same session came the first of several schemes for a railway to Godstone – the Caterham & Godstone Railway. It was to be an extension from the Caterham (South-Eastern) terminus, through two short tunnels under Tupwood, at a gradient of 1 in 40, to the summit of Godstone Hill, and through two more tunnels to Godstone. Nothing further was heard of this scheme.

Two years later there came a more ambitious scheme, the Metropolitan & Brighton Railway, which was to leave the London, Chatham & Dover near Penge, and the South-Eastern near Beckenham, passing thence through Farley, Warlingham village, Caterham, Godstone, East Grinstead, and thence to Brighton *via* Lindfield and Clayton. The ruling gradient was to be 1 in 100, and the engineering works included a viaduct of 364 yards over the Woldingham Valley road; a tunnel under Tillingdown, 368 yards long, emerging into Caterham Valley not far from the present station; and a further tunnel under Godstone Hill. The line was to be connected by loops to the South-Eastern main line at Godstone. One wonders in what way the development of Caterham would have been affected if it had been served by a main line to Brighton.

In the following year, another abortive scheme, the Caterham &

[1]Ordnance Survey Map, 25 in. to mile, 1867–8.

Godstone Valley, was projected, but did at least get an Act of incorporation;[1] it was to run on a similar, if slightly easier, gradient to Godstone and Oxted, with an extension to Westerham to join the proposed Westerham Valley Railway. A later projection was for the Godstone Village Extension Railway, from Godstone Corner to a station in Godstone at Tyler's Green. Although this line remained on paper for several years, and the South-Eastern authorised the expenditure of £40,000 on it, the scheme came to nothing. This was chiefly owing to the resuscitation of the Surrey & Sussex Junction as the Croydon, Oxted & East Grinstead,[2] which would very nearly have paralleled its course. There is also a local story that the quarrying under Godstone Hill would have proved dangerous for major tunnelling operations. The only sign of railway activity in the district was the building of the Corner House at Godstone, which was intended as the Station Hotel.

In 1882 came the wildest scheme of all, the Coulsdon & Upper Caterham Railway. This remarkable line was, like the South Caterham, quite clear as to its starting point, which was to be measured from 'the south-western corner of the south-eastern parapet of the Godstone-road bridge' at Caterham Junction. It was to run alongside the Brighton to near Stoat's Nest, whence it was to follow a similar course to the South Caterham, the main difference being that, while that line was to terminate in Upper Caterham village, the Coulsdon & Upper Caterham was to terminate about a mile beyond, at a point on Willey Heath where there was no habitation at all. Needless to say, this odd proposal died a natural death. That local people were the promoters seems obvious, but to build a line more or less to one's own back door was adventurous in the extreme.

Still one more scheme could be added to this list: the Upper Caterham Railway, leaving the Brighton line near the present Coulsdon South station, and following the valley parallel to, and east of, Farthing Downs, ended in the dip where Roffe's lane joins the Chaldon-Caterham road. It appears that a light track was laid on this route in the 'seventies, during the construction of the Guards' Depot at Caterham.

[1]13 July 1876.
[2]Opened 10 March 1884.

The official seal of the Caterham Railway Company.

Chapter Eight

Improvements (1890–1928)

Until the 'nineties the Caterham district remained in a half-developed state, but the spread of housing most of the way down the Caterham valley, and the building of a number of shops, induced the South-Eastern to begin considering proposals for improvements, and in July 1890 their Engineer was directed to prepare plans and an estimate for the widening of the line.

In November 1892 Caterham residents asked for points and cross-over roads to be put in at the north end of Purley station, to enable trains to run through to London without shunting.

By 1895, plans were in hand for widening the line, though it is surprising to find a tender accepted for the painting of Caterham (old) station, including a signboard with painting and writing of ''GENTLEMEN', the latter to cost about £1, 'if done'. One hopes that it was.[1]

Developments were hastened by the incorporation, under South-Eastern auspices, of a line since closely linked with the Caterham line. This was the Chipstead Valley Railway, incorporated 1893, as a line from Purley to Walton-on-the-Hill, and the Epsom Downs Extension to Tattenham Corner. The Agreements between the South-Eastern and Brighton must have faded from the mind, for the area west of the main line should have been a Brighton stronghold, especially as that Company's branch from Sutton to Epsom Downs catered for the Epsom Race Meetings.[2] With an eye to securing some of this valuable traffic, the South-Eastern decided that Tattenham Corner, even if further from London in mileage, was in a superior position for the racecourse. The Chipstead Valley was opened to Kingswood on 2 November 1897, to Tadworth & Walton-on-the-Hill on 1 July 1900, and to Tattenham Corner on 4 June 1901.[3] Work of reconstruction on the Caterham branch included doubling the line (i.e. the addition of the 'up' line). The whole track was slewed about all over the place; for instance, the down side at Warlingham was the new side. A new station was to be opened at Whyteleafe, and a newer and larger station at Caterham. The new Caterham station necessitated the raising of the Station Avenue several feet, which must have afforded relief from the flooding which periodically inundated the town from the streams of water pouring off the hills.

---

[1]SER Minutes, 23 March 1895.

[2]The Brighton automatically opposed the scheme, but without any real success.

[3]Until the Autumn of 1907, Tattenham Corner had a regular service of trains, the South-Eastern & Chatham, as it had then become, wishing to develop an excursion traffic to Epsom Downs. This project failed, either through lack of advertising on the part of the railway company, or lack of interest in Epsom Downs on the part of the public. Until electrification, Tadworth was used as the terminus, Tattenham Corner being used only on race days or for specials.

LONDON, EAST CROYDON, PURLEY, and CATERHAM.—South Eastern and Chatham.

Miles	Down.	Week Days.															
		mrn	mrn	mrn	mrn	mrn Except Saturdays.	mrn Sats. only.	mrn	mrn	aft Sats. only.	aft Except Saturdays.	aft Saturdays only.	aft Sats. only.	aft Sats. only.	aft Sats. only.	aft Sats. only.	aft Except Saturdays.
	Charing Cross ....dep.	5 15	6 50	....	....	9 24	9 40	1050	1145	....	1250	1255	1 21	....	....	....	2 5
¾	Waterloo Junction	5 17	6 52	....	....	....	....	1052	1147	....	1252	1257	1 23	....	....	....	2 7
—	Cannon Street	5 25	7 0	7 54	....	....	....	11 0	....	1242	1 0	1 2	....	1 30	....	2 12	2 14
1¾	London Bridge	5 32	7 8	7 57	9b10	9 30	....	11 5	1153	1245	1 7	1 7	1 30	1 32	1b51	2 15	2 19
12¼	East Croydon	5 55	7 30	8 20	9 27	9 53	....	1126	1212	1 4	1 28	1 28	1 49	1 56	2 7	2 38	2 40
15¼	Purley 257 .... arr.	6 3	7 38	8 29	9 34	10 2	10 8	1135	1220	1 11	1 36	1 36	1 56	2 4	2 14	2 44	2 48
	dep.	6 8	7 42	8 44	9 38	1010	1012	1141	1224	1 12	1 41	1 41	1 57	2 5	2 16	2 48	2 53
16¼	Kenley, for Riddlesdown	6 11	7 45	8 47	9 41	1013	1015	1144	1227	1 15	1 44	1 44	....	2 8	2 21	2 51	2 56
17¼	Whyteleafe	6 16	7 50	8 52	9 46	1018	1020	1149	1232	1 20	1 49	....	....	2 13	2 26	....	3 1
18¼	Warlingham	6 19	7 53	8 55	9 49	1021	1023	1152	1235	1 23	1 52	1 49	....	2 16	2 29	2 56	3 4
19¾	Caterham ....arr.	6 24	7 58	9 0	9 51	1026	1028	1157	1240	1 28	1 57	1 54	2 5	2 21	2 34	3 1	3 9

Down.	Week Days—Continued.																
	aft	aft	aft	aft	aft Sats. only.	aft	aft Except Saturdays.	aft Sats. only.	aft Except Saturdays.	aft Except Saturdays.	aft Sats. only.	aft Except Saturdays.	aft Except Saturdays.	aft	aft Sats. only.	aft Except Saturdays.	aft
Charing Cross ....dep.	2s12	....	....	3 8	3 47	....	4 20	4 20	....	....	5 15	5 15	....	6 5	6 22	6 35	....
Waterloo Junction	....	....	....	3 10	3 49	....	....	4 22	....	....	5 17	5 17	....	....	6 24	....	....
Cannon Street	....	....	3s4	3 18	....	4e12	4 29	4 29	....	....	5 24	5 26	....	6 13	6 30	....	6e45
London Bridge	2s18	2b50	3s6	3 21	3 55	4e15	4 35	4 35	4b52	5b20	5 29	5 31	5b54	6 17	6 35	6 41	6e50
East Croydon	2s43	3 6	3s27	3 43	....	4e34	4 55	4 55	....	....	5 51	5 53	6 11	6 39	6 54	6 59	7e10
Purley 257 .... arr.	2s51	3 13	3s34	3 52	4 18	4e41	5 2	5 2	5 13	5 42	5 58	6 1	6 18	6 47	7 0	7 6	7e17
dep.	3s0	3s14	3s38	3 57	4 22	4e45	5 6	5 6	5 17	5 43	6 2	6 5	6 22	6 48	7 4	7 7	7 21
Kenley, for Riddlesdown....	3s3	3s17	3s41	4 0	4 25	4e48	5 9	5 9	5 20	5 46	6 7	6 10	6 25	6 51	7 7	....	7 24
Whyteleafe	....	3s22	3s46	4 5	4 30	4e53	....	5 13	5 24	5 50	6 12	6 15	....	6 56	7 12	....	....
Warlingham	3s8	3s26	3s49	4 8	4 33	4e56	5 14	5 16	5 27	5 53	6 15	6 18	6 30	6 59	7 15	7 13	7 29
Caterham ....arr.	3s13	3s31	3s54	4 13	4 38	5e1	5 19	5 21	5 32	5 58	6 20	6 23	6 35	7 4	7 20	7 18	7 34

Down.	Week Days—Continued.								Sundays.												
	aft Except Saturdays.	aft	aft Except Saturdays.	aft	aft	aft	aft	aft	mrn	mrn	mrn	mrn	aft	aft	aft	aft	aft	aft	aft	aft	aft
Charing Cross ....dep.	....	7 16	7 55	8 43	....	10 3	1037	1140	7 22	....	9 15	1015	1258	2 30	....	5 30	7 0	....	8 50	9 35	11 2
Waterloo Junction	....	7 18	7 57	8 45	....	10 5	....	....	7 24	....	....	1017	1 0	2 32	....	5 32	7 2	....	8 52	9 37	11 4
Cannon Street	....	7 26	8 2	8 53	....	....	1045	....	7 31	....	....	1025	....	....	....	5 40	....	....	8 59	....	....
London Bridge	7b15	7 30	8 7	8 57	....	1010	1048	1146	7 36	....	9 20	1027	1 5	2 37	....	5 44	7 8	....	9 2	9 42	1110
East Croydon	7 34	7 53	8 25	9 17	....	1031	11 7	12 7	7 57	....	9 37	1048	1 25	2 55	....	6 5	7 27	....	9 22	10 2	1130
Purley 257 .... arr.	7 41	8 2	8 32	9 24	....	1039	1114	1214	8 4	....	9 44	1056	1 32	3 2	....	6 13	7 34	....	9 30	10 9	1137
dep.	7 42	8 6	8 36	9 27	1027	1043	1118	1218	8 8	8 51	9 48	11 1	1 36	3 12	5 27	6 17	7 38	8 37	9 38	1015	1141
Kenley, for Riddlesdown....	7 45	8 9	8 39	9 30	....	1046	1121	1221	8 11	8 54	9 51	11 4	1 39	3 15	5 30	6 20	7 41	8 40	9 41	1018	1144
Whyteleafe	7 50	8 14	8 43	9 35	....	1051	1126	1226	....	8 58	9 55	11 8	1 43	3 19	5 34	6 24	7 45	8 44	9 45	1022	1148
Warlingham	7 53	8 17	8 46	9 38	1033	1054	1129	1229	8 16	9 1	9 58	1111	1 46	3 22	5 37	6 27	7 48	8 47	9 48	1025	1152
Caterham ....arr.	7 58	8 22	8 51	9 43	1038	1059	1134	1234	8 21	9 6	10 3	1116	1 51	3 27	5 42	6 32	7 53	8 52	9 53	1030	1157

Miles	Up.	Week Days.																				
		mrn	mrn	mrn		mrn	mrn		mrn	mrn	mrn	mrn	mrn		mrn	aft	aft	aft	aft		aft Sats. only.	aft Except Saturdays.
	Caterham ....dep.	5 17	7 20	8 6	....	8 27	8 40	....	8 57	9 12	9 38	9 56	1041	....	1114	12 1	1 11	2 0	2 59	....	3 31	3 33
1½	Warlingham	5 20	7 23	8 9	....	8 31	8 43	....	9 1	....	9 41	9 59	1044	....	1117	12 4	1 14	2 3	3 2	....	3 34	3 36
2¼	Whyteleafe	5 22	7 25	8 11	....	8 34	8 45	....	9 4	....	9 43	10 2	1047	....	1120	12 7	1 17	2 6	3 5	....	3 37	3 39
3¾	Kenley, for Riddlesdown	5 26	7 29	8 15	....	8 38	8 49	....	9 8	....	9 47	10 6	1051	....	1124	1211	1 21	2 10	3 9	....	3 41	3 43
4½	Purley 257, 262 .. arr.	5 30	7 33	8 19	....	8 42	8 53	....	9 12	9 19	9 51	1010	1055	....	1128	1215	1 25	2 14	3 13	....	3 45	3 48
	dep.	....	7 36	8 20	....	8 43	9 1	....	9 13	9 20	9 53	1011	1057	....	1131	1218	1 28	2 17	3 16	....		4 0
7¼	East Croydon	....	7 43	8 29	....	8 48	9 7	....	9 20	9 27	9 59	1017	11 3	....	1138	1224	1 34	2 23	3 23	....		4 7
18	London Bridge	....	8 0	8 46	....	9 5	9b24	....	9 37	9 45	1016	1036	1121	....	1158	1243	1b51	2 42	3 42	....		4 24
18½	Cannon Street	....	8 6	8 50	....	9 9	....	....	9 41	9 49	1020	1040	....	....	12e4	1247	....	2 47	3 46	....		....
19	Waterloo Junction	....	8 13	8 56	....	....	....	....	9 48	....	1026	....	1126	....	1210	1254	....	2 55	....	....		4 30
19½	Charing Cross ....arr.	....	8 17	9 0	....	....	....	....	9 52	....	1030	....	1130	....	1214	1258	....	2 59	....	....		4 34

Up.	Week Days—Continued.										
	aft	aft	aft	aft Sats. only.	aft Sats. only.	aft	aft	aft	aft	aft	aft
Caterham ....dep.	4 42	5 16	6 13	6 30	6 50	7 43	8 51	9 18	10 6	1055	1111
Warlingham	4 45	5 19	6 16	6 33	6 53	7 46	8 54	9 21	10 9	1058	1114
Whyteleafe	4 48	5 22	6 19	6 36	6 58	7 49	8 57	9 24	1012	11 1	1117
Kenley, for Riddlesdown	4 52	5 26	6 23	6 40	7 0	7 53	9 1	9 28	1016	11 5	1122
Purley 257, 262 .... arr.	4 56	5 30	6 27	6 44	7 4	7 57	9 5	9 32	1020	11 9	1126
dep.	4 59	5 33	6 30	6 45	7 7	8 7	9 8	9 33	....	1114	....
East Croydon	5 7	5 40	6 37	6 50	7 14	8 14	9 15	9 39	....	1120	....
London Bridge	5 25	5 58	6 55	7 8	7 34	8 33	9 32	9 57	....	1137	....
Cannon Street	....	....	7 6	....	....	8 38	9 37	10 1	....	....	....
Waterloo Junction	5 31	6 5	7 7	7 14	7 39	8 45	9 46	....	....	1143	....
Charing Cross ....arr.	5 35	6 9	7 11	7 18	7 43	8 49	9 50	....	....	1147	....

Up.	Sundays.												
	mrn	mrn	mrn	mrn	aft	aft	aft	aft	aft	aft	aft	aft	aft
Caterham ....dep.	7 46	8 27	9 23	1015	1 14	2 46	5 0	5 52	6 41	8 15	9 15	9 58	1110
Warlingham	7 49	8 30	9 26	1018	1 17	2 49	5 3	5 55	6 44	8 18	9 18	10 1	1113
Whyteleafe	7 52	[illegible]	9 29	1021	1 20	2 52	5 6	5 58	6 47	8 21	9 21	....	....
Kenley, for Riddlesdown	7 56	8 3[illegible]	9 33	1025	1 24	2 56	5 10	6 2	6 51	8 25	9 25	....	1118
Purley 257, 263 .... arr.	8 0	8 39	9 37	1029	1 28	3 0	5 14	6 6	6 55	8 29	9 29	10 8	1122
dep.	....	8 41	....	1036	....	3 9	5 21	6 12	6 58	8 35	9 40	....	....
East Croydon	....	8 49	....	1043	....	3 16	5 27	6 17	7 6	8 41	9 47	....	....
London Bridge	....	9 7	....	11 1	....	3 33	5 44	6 34	7 24	8 58	10 7	....	....
Cannon Street	....	9 12	....	11 7	....	....	5 48	....	....	....	1011	....	....
Waterloo Junction	....	9 19	....	1114	....	3 38	5 55	6 40	7 31	9 3	1018	....	....
Charing Cross ....arr.	....	9 24	....	1118	....	3 42	6 0	6 44	7 35	9 7	1022	....	....

NOTES.

b London Bridge (Low Level Station).
e Except Saturdays.
s Saturdays only.

☞ For other Trains BETWEEN London and Purley PAGE ...262

London and Caterham time-table taken from *Bradshaw*, 1911.

In December 1895, the Brighton was asked to carry out the necessary improvements at Purley: a double junction with the main line, a new platform, and a Booking Office on the down side. The estimated cost of this was over £12,000. The new Purley Engine Shed, built by the South-Eastern, cost in all nearly £10,000. Purchase of land on the branch came to more than the latter amount. The whole Caterham scheme amounted to about £75,000.[1]

Work started in 1897, and was completed by 1 January 1900. Whyteleafe station was opened on that day. During this period of reconstruction a platform known as Halliloo,[2] situated on the north side of Burntwood Bridge, was removed. It was used chiefly by parties of schoolchildren, but never appeared in a time-table.

Control of traffic to and from Caterham and Chipstead Valley was transferred to a new signal-box at Purley East. This was closed down when the railway was electrified, but the top of the box remained in use as a hut for many years. And the new Purley Box of 1955, built in the fork between the Chipstead Valley and the main line, and which replaced Purley North and Purley South boxes, lay in total ruin in July 1985.

The train service of the 'nineties, though on the whole adequate, required some improvement. There were fifteen trains up and down on weekdays, almost all of which connected with trains to or from London, four (five on Saturdays) running through. On Sundays there were five up and six down trains. In a number of cases the connexions could hardly be described as good, a twenty minutes to half-an-hour wait being not uncommon. In one or two cases, the Brighton Company's trains left Purley at the same minute as the Caterham train was due to arrive. This must have been galling to would-be passengers, but one should not, perhaps, blame the Brighton for this. Relations with the South-Eastern over the use of the Redhill-Croydon section had become even more difficult than in the past. It was always touch and go which train got through first at Redhill, and deliberate hold-ups were not unknown. Whatever the Brighton did, the South-Eastern made a nuisance of itself, or *vice versa*.[3] Consequently, punctuality anywhere between London and Redhill was a matter of some concern to passengers. The Brighton, tiring of endless broken Agreements over the use of this section,[4] extended its suburban line – two extra tracks – from South Croydon to Stoat's Nest on 5 November 1899, and from there to Earlswood, avoiding Redhill, on 1 April 1900.

---

[1]SER Reports and Accounts.

[2]Halliloo is a farm in Woldingham, some distance away.

[3]One case in particular was the 6 pm down from London Bridge to Redhill and Brighton, which was followed by the South-Eastern's 6.01 pm put on more for the sake of pigheadedness than anything else.

[4]It would be unfair to suppose that the South-Eastern or the Brighton was always in the wrong; very often it was just 'incompatibility of temperament'.

London and Caterham.] 253 [S. E. & C.

LONDON, EAST CROYDON, PURLEY, and CATERHAM.—South Eastern and Chatham.

Down. — Week Days.

Miles	Down.		mrn	mrn	mrn	mrn	mrn	mrn	mrn	aft	aft	aft	aft	aft	aft	aft	aft	aft	aft
									Sats. only.	Except Saturdays.	Sats. only.			Sats. only.	Sats. only.	Except Saturdays.	Sats. only.		
—	Charing Cross	dep.	....	....	....	....	....	10 55	....		....	1255	....	....	....	2 3	....	2s35	3 3
¾	Waterloo Junction		....	....	....	....	....	....	....		....	1257	....	....	....	2 5	....	....	....
—	Cannon Street		4 45	....	....	....	....	....	11 40		1240	....	....	1 18	....	....	....	....	....
1¾	London Bridge		5 0	....	7b48	9b13	....	11 2	11 43		1243	1 4	12b54	1 22	1b30	2 10	2b22	2s41	3 10
12¾	East Croydon		5 19	....	8 6	9 31	....	11 24	12 4		1 2	1 24	1 11	1 41	2 3	2 31	2 41	3s 1	3 30
15½	Purley 268	arr.	5 29	....	8 14	9 39	....	11 34	12 12		1 9	1 32	1 18	1 49	2 15	2 40	2 51	3s 9	3 38
		dep.	5 45	7 0	8 45	9 42	1045	11 41	12 18	1230	1 11	1 40	Sats. only.	1 52	2 20	2 46	2 57	3 24	3 45
16½	Kenley		5 47	7 2	8 48	9 45	1048	11 44	12 21	1233	1 14	1 43		1 55	2 23	2 49	3 0	3 27	3 48
17½	Whyteleafe		5 53	7 7	8 53	9 50	1053	11 49	12 26	1238	1 19	1 48		2 0	2 28	2 54	3 5	3 32	3 53
18¼	Warlingham		5 56	7 10	8 56	9 53	1056	11 52	12 29	1241	1 22	1 51		2 3	2 31	2 57	3 8	3 35	3 56
19¾	Caterham	arr.	6 1	7 15	9 1	9 58	11 1	11 57	12 34	1246	1 27	1 56		2 8	2 36	3 2	3 13	3 40	4 1

Down. — Week Days—Continued.

Down.		aft	aft	aft	aft	aft	aft	aft	aft	aft	aft	aft	aft	aft	aft	aft	aft
		Except Sats.	Except Saturdays.	Sats. only.	Except Saturdays.	Except Saturdays.	Except Sats.	Sats. only.	Except Saturdays.	Except Saturdays.							
Charing Cross	dep.		....	4 22	....	5 6	....	5 30	5 30	....	6s17	6e46	7s24	8 28	9 25	1017	1128
Waterloo Junction			....	....	....	5 8	....	....	5 32	....	....	6e48	....	....	....	....	....
Cannon Street			4 24	....	4 44	....	....	....	....	....	6e20	....	7e28	....	....	....	....
London Bridge			4 28	4 28	4 48	5 14	5b33	5 36	5 37	5b48	6 23	6e53	7 30	8 36	9 31	1023	....
East Croydon			4 48	4 48	....	5 36	5 51	5 55	5 55	6 8	6s42	7e12	7 50	8 56	9 51	1042	1149
Purley 268	arr.		4 55	4 56	5 13	5 43	5 58	6 2	6 3	6 16	6 47	7e20	7 58	9 4	10 0	1051	1158
	dep.	4 40	5 1	5 2	5 18	5 45	Except Sats.	6 4	6 5	6 21	6 49	7 25	8 5	9 11	10 6	1058	12 5
Kenley		4 43	5 4	5 5	5 21	5 48		6 7	6 8	6 23	6 52	7 28	8 8	9 14	10 9	11 1	12 8
Whyteleafe		4 48	5 9	5 10	5 26	5 53		6 12	6 13	6 28	6 57	7 32	8 13	9 19	1014	11 6	1213
Warlingham		4 51	5 12	5 13	5 29	5 55		6 15	6 16	6 31	7 1	7 35	8 16	9 22	1017	11 9	1216
Caterham	arr.	4 56	5 17	5 18	5 34	6 0		6 19	6 20	6 36	7 7	7 40	8 21	9 27	1022	1114	1221

Down. — Sundays.

Down.		mrn	mrn	mrn	mrn	aft	aft	aft	aft	aft	aft	aft	aft
Charing Cross	dep.	6 40	....	9 8	1020	....	1 30	....	5 32	7 5	....	8 45	9 40
Waterloo Junction		a	....	....	1022	....	1 32	....	5 34	7 8	....	8 48	9 42
Cannon Street		....	....	....	....	....	....	....	....	....	....	....	....
London Bridge		6 48	....	9 14	1029	....	1 37	....	5 40	7 13	....	8 55	9 47
East Croydon		7 11	....	9 32	1049	....	1 57	....	6 0	7 33	....	9 15	10 7
Purley 268	arr.	7 21	....	9 39	1053	....	2 5	....	6 8	7 41	....	9 24	1016
	dep.	7 31	8 55	9 43	11 8	12 5	2 11	4 5	6 14	7 46	8 37	9 30	1022
Kenley		7 34	8 58	9 46	1111	12 8	2 14	4 8	6 17	7 49	8 40	9 33	1025
Whyteleafe		....	9 2	9 50	1115	1212	2 18	4 12	6 21	7 53	8 45	9 38	1029
Warlingham		7 39	9 5	9 53	1118	1215	2 21	4 15	6 24	7 56	8 48	9 41	1032
Caterham	arr.	7 44	9 10	9 58	1123	1220	2 26	4 20	6 29	8 1	8 53	9 46	1037

Up. — Week Days.

Miles	Up.		mrn	mrn	mrn	mrn	mrn	mrn	mrn	mrn	mrn	mrn	aft	aft	aft	aft	aft	aft	aft	aft	aft	aft	aft
—	Caterham	dep.	7 19	7 47	8 1	8 24	8 35	8 57	9 10	9 39	1015	10 45	12 5	1 16	2 59	3 22	4 12	5 27	6 30	7 43	8 20	9 12	1111
1½	Warlingham		7 22	7 51	8 5	8 28	8 39	9 0	....	9 42	1018	10 48	12 8	1 19	3 2	3 25	4 15	5 30	6 33	7 46	8 23	9 15	1114
2¼	Whyteleafe		7 24	7 53	8 7	8 30	8 41	9 3	....	9 44	1021	10 51	12 11	1 22	3 5	3 28	4 18	5 33	6 36	7 49	8 26	9 18	1117
3¼	Kenley		7 28	7 57	8 11	8 34	8 45	9 7	....	9 48	1025	10 55	12 15	1 26	3 9	3 32	4 22	5 37	6 40	7 53	8 30	9 22	1121
4¼	Purley 172, 244, 268	arr.	7 32	8 1	8 15	8 38	8 49	9 11	9 18	9 52	1029	10 59	12 19	1 30	3 13	3 36	4 26	5 40	6 44	7 57	8 34	9 26	1125
		dep.	7 34	8 4	8 17	8 40	8 57	9 12	9 21	9 55	1037	11 11	12 23	1 32	3 16	....	4 33	5 42	6 54	8 0	8 37	9 38	1135
7¾	East Croydon		7 41	8 10	8 23	8 47	9 3	9 19	9 27	10 0	1043	11 19	12 31	1 38	3 24	....	4 40	5 51	7 2	8 5	8 44	9 45	1148
18	London Bridge		7 58	8 28	8 40	9 4	9 22	9 40	9b45	1018	11b0	11 37	12 50	1 56	3 42	....	4 58	6 10	7 20	8 23	9 2	10 8	12 1
18¾	Cannon Street		....	8 32	8 44	9 8	....	9 44	....	1022	....	....	....	....	....	....	....	....	....	....	....	....	....
19	Waterloo Junction		8 3	....	....	....	9 27	....	....	....	....	11 44	12 56	....	....	....	5 8	6 15	....	8 28	9 11	....	....
19¾	Charing Cross	arr.	8 7	....	....	....	9 31	....	....	....	....	11 48	1 0	2 5	3s49	....	5 14	6 19	7 30	8 32	9 15	10 13	1210

Up. — Sundays.

Up.		mrn	mrn	mrn	mrn	mrn	aft	aft	aft	aft	aft	h	aft
Caterham	dep.	7 0	8 0	9 23	1035	1136	1 45	3 45	5 44	6 38	8 15	9 4	10 0
Warlingham		7 3	8 3	9 26	1039	1139	1 48	3 49	5 47	6 41	8 18	9 7	10 3
Whyteleafe		7 6	....	9 29	1042	1142	1 51	3 52	5 50	6 44	8 21	9 10	....
Kenley		7 10	8 8	9 33	1046	1146	1 55	3 56	5 54	6 48	8 25	9 14	....
Purley 176, 245, 268	arr.	7 14	8 12	9 37	1050	1150	1 59	4 0	5 58	6 52	8 29	9 18	1010
	dep.	....	8 15	....	11 8	....	....	4 9	6 8	6 57	8 38	9 46	....
East Croydon		....	8 22	....	1112	....	....	4 15	6 13	7 5	8 43	9 53	....
London Bridge		....	8 40	....	1131	....	....	4 33	6 30	7 23	9 1	1012	....
Cannon Street		....	....	....	....	....	....	....	....	....	....	....	....
Waterloo Junction		....	....	....	1140	....	....	4 38	6 35	7 30	....	....	....
Charing Cross	arr.	....	8 49	....	1144	....	....	4 42	6 39	7 34	9 9	1022	....

a Calls at Norwood Junction at 7 6 mrn.

b London Bridge (Low Level Station).

e Except Saturdays.

h Calls at Norwood Junction at 10 1 aft.

s Saturdays only.

For other Trains

BETWEEN PAGE

London and Purley 172, 193, 206, 244

London and Caterham time-table taken from *Bradshaw*, 1922.

Forty-five minutes was normally allowed for the journey from or to Caterham and London Bridge, but an extra quarter-of-an-hour was taken to get to Charing Cross, owing to the system of running most trains into and out of Cannon Street *en route*.

This easy-going period was also marked by the presence of a locally famous pair of enginemen, father and son, driver and fireman, who took on the duties of the Caterham branch. The exploits of this pair are still spoken of with cheerful good will, for the licensing hours were different in those days, and the bars of the Railway Hotels at Caterham and Purley were hospitable and convenient, and open all day; and there was usually enough time at both ends for refreshment. The only result of this happy-go-lucky attitude was the damage done, on one occasion, to the level-crossing gates at Whyteleafe, and an unexpected departure from normal routine which gave an unusual, if impressive, spectacle to passengers and passers-by, of a train careering through the buffer stops at Caterham and up the bank into the road.[1]

The legendary 'cow on the line' happened to be true on the Caterham branch, for Driver George Whickman had once to chase a cow most of the way from Whyteleafe to Kenley.

In November 1899, the South-Eastern & Chatham[2] embarked on a new scheme to provide Caterham and Chipstead Valley with a direct service from London over the Mid-Kent line. An Act was acquired on 6 August 1900 to build a line from near Sanderstead to a junction with the Caterham branch, between Purley and Kenley; and a line to the right to join on to the Chipstead Valley line by the LB&SC bridge over that line. By this date, the Brighton had taken all the available land in the vicinity of Purley station, so that any attempt to squeeze a line through between the station and Purley Downs was out of the question. Consequently a tunnel of 580 yards was necessary to penetrate the Downs, with a new Purley Junction station. A new bridge over the Godstone Road was also required, and was to be 'of a width or span of 40 feet at the least'. It was unfortunate that this line never got further than the planning stage, as in the present troublesome conditions of overcrowding, it might have proved very useful.

From 1 January 1900, the new service included about half a dozen extra trains, and alterations in times of others, which provided better connexions with main line trains. The South-Eastern had realised, rather belatedly, that the public was deserving of some consideration. Thus encouraged, the district began to develop more rapidly. The nucleus of houses and small shops, centred chiefly round the station, began to spread outwards. Towards the end of 1903, a 'fast' train to

[1]This is a local legend: there is no mention of it in official Accident Reports.

[2]The South-Eastern and the London, Chatham & Dover Railways formed a Joint Managing Committee in 1899.

London was included in the time-table. This left Caterham at 9.12 am and, stopping only at Purley and East Croydon, arrived at London Bridge at 9.45 am – two minutes faster than the best time in 1952. It is, perhaps, of no more than academic interest that the fastest timing now (1985) between Caterham and London Bridge is 34 minutes; curiously enough it is the timing for the 9.20 am, which was also the time of the departure which superseded the old 9.12 as a 'fast' in 1928. Most trains take much longer. From Mondays to Fridays, at 6.42 pm, and on Saturdays at 1.30 pm, a similar train left London Bridge for Caterham. This continued for a number of years. The up train lasted until shortly after electrification, and was considered to be the wealthy business man's train, and rather exclusive. An elderly gentleman remarked, not so long ago, that 'in those days, Sir, it was considered indecent for more than two people to travel in a first-class compartment'.

Caterham's train services have been in the habit of getting into a rut for long periods at a time. As the period from the 'sixties to 1900 remained more or less static, so too did the period from 1900 until electrification in 1928. The First World War made little difference until January 1917, when reductions were made on all lines. Caterham services were cut down to a certain extent; some business trains did not run on Saturdays, and a number of trains in the slack period were cancelled. All the stations on the branch remained open, though on the Tadworth branch, both Smitham and Reedham Halt were closed; the vast building development in this area had not then begun.[1]

With the return to more normal conditions came a somewhat better service. Indeed, during the latter part of the steam *régime*, that is, in the early nineteen-twenties, the business service was in some respects better than a quarter of a century later, when one considers the rise in population. At the 1923 grouping, when the SE&C, LB&SC and L&SW Railways formed the Southern Railway, the Caterham and Chipstead Valley branches were transferred to the Central (Brighton) Section.

Since the grouping, and with the more general use of motor-cars and bus services, there has been a tendency for people from outlying districts to use Caterham station, owing to a generally better commuter service, and even a better service during off-peak times. Caterham itself is by no means a compact town, but spread over a wide area and joining on, in several directions, to the huge sprawling mass of London suburbia. Godstone commuters find it easier to use Caterham than their own station, several miles in the opposite direction. At one time there was a comparatively heavy traffic from the Guards'

[1]Even up to electrification, the last down train arrived at Reedham Halt at 9.57 pm and at Smitham at 10 pm, except on Wednesdays and Saturdays. The last up train at both stations was shortly after 8 o'clock.

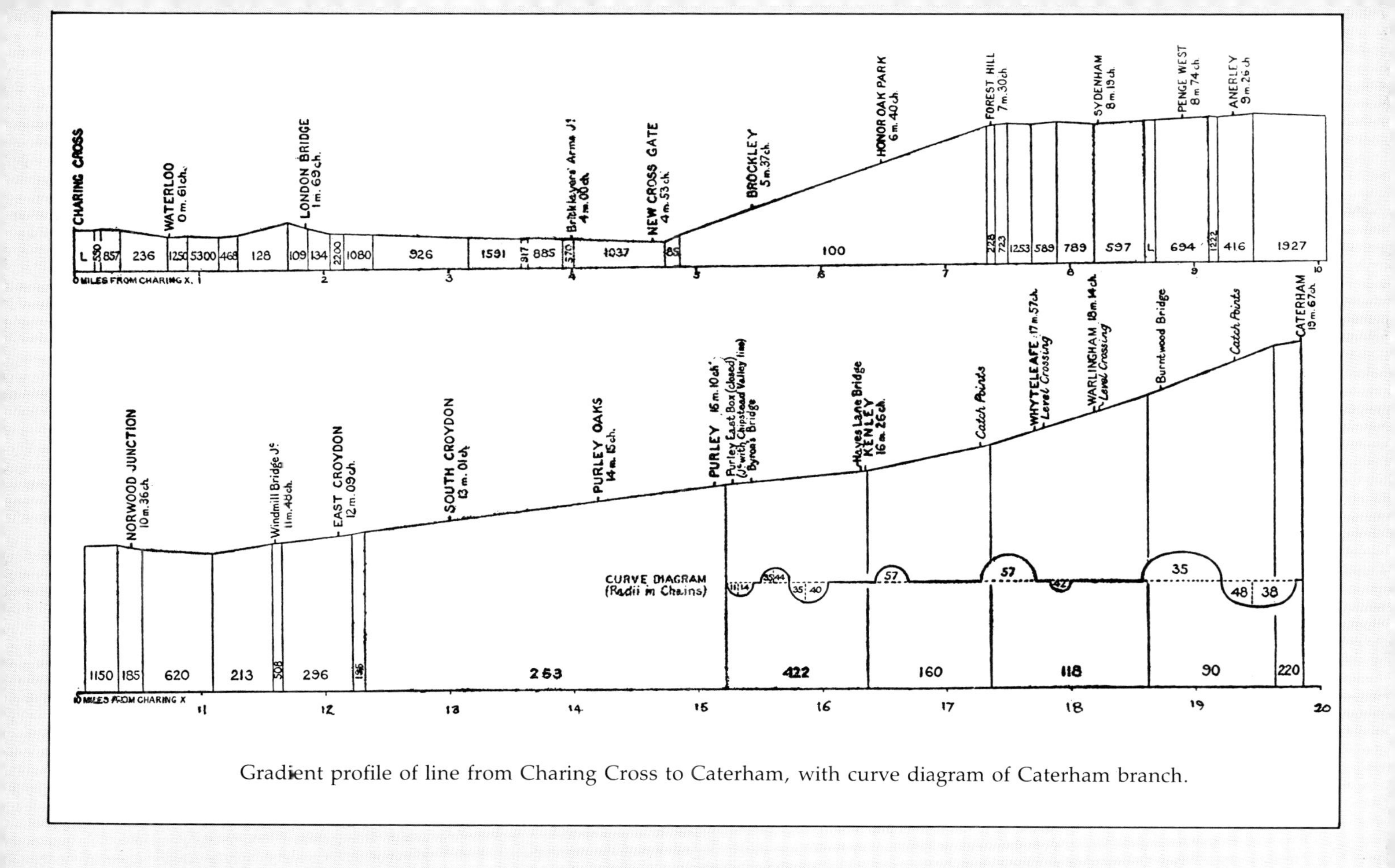

Gradient profile of line from Charing Cross to Caterham, with curve diagram of Caterham branch.

Depot, but guardsmen now have cars. Whyteleafe once served Kenley Aerodrome, a not inconsiderable traffic that has now ceased.

The down business service of the steam days, though less frequent than the electric, was more convenient for those whose work took them to the area round Charing Cross and Cannon Street, for a number of trains ran through during business hours. That these ceased to do so on electrification was no fault of the Southern Railway, whose General Manager, Sir Herbert Walker, pointed it out in a letter at the time, apologising for the fact that all business trains from Caterham and Tattenham Corner would terminate at London Bridge low level platforms. The congestion already in evidence between London Bridge and Cannon Street and Charing Cross would clearly have been worsened by attempting to find paths for many extra trains. Apart from congestion west of London Bridge, down trains would, of course, have fouled the tracks of up trains from the Dartford lines, and the Company wisely, if inconveniently, debarred Caterham trains during rush hours west of London Bridge. The system of running separate Caterham and Tadworth trains during rush hours disappeared after electrification, and all trains were joined and divided at Purley.

Caterham station in the 1920s. *Lens of Sutton*

Chapter Nine

Electrification and after

Until the electrification of the Caterham and Chipstead Valley branches, the London Bridge to East Croydon section was used wholly by steam services. Beyond this point, electric services on the overhead system had been running to Coulsdon North, on the local line only, since 1 April 1925. In order to electrify this steam section, and deal with the heavy business traffic to and from Croydon and Purley, it was necessary to find a convenient terminal point beyond this congested area. Caterham and Tattenham Corner were ideal for the purpose, and the Southern Railway, with a go-ahead policy of developing an intense service on suburban lines, decided that electrification of these branches would in part fulfil their objective. At the same time, steps were taken to convert the Coulsdon North trains from overhead system to third rail. Also included in the general scheme was electrification of the Sydenham to Crystal Palace (Low Level) Branch. Additional rolling-stock was required for these purposes, and 116 three-coach units and 47 two-coach trailer units were adapted. Many of these coaches were South-Eastern four- and six-wheelers, two of which were joined together on a new underframe to form an eight-wheel coach. A number of them were to be seen until recently running on Caterham and Chipstead Valley trains; some still had luggage rack supports embellished with the initials 'S.E.R', which indicated that the body was of considerable age. Each motor-coach was equipped with two 275 hp motors of the totally-enclosed, self-ventilating type. Sub-stations, fed by the main power station at Lewisham, were built at Forest Hill, Norwood Fork, Purley, Kingswood and Warlingham. Longer platforms were required at Reedham Halt, Chipstead and Kingswood on the Tattenham branch, and at Warlingham on the Caterham branch.

At Purley little structural alteration was necessary, except for the lengthening of the down Caterham and Tattenham platform (No. 6) to accommodate a nine-coach train, 582 feet in length, with seating capacity of over 700. Certain signalling alterations were also necessary here, to enable the two portions to join up.

Trailer units were not formed in Caterham and Chipstead Valley trains (except for Tattenham Corner race specials) and only three-car 'sets' were available. Owing to the disproportionate quota of first-class accommodation needed on the Chipstead Valley branch, it was decided to form two three-coach sets for Chipstead Valley, and one three-coach set for Caterham, to make up a nine-coach train during business hours. This meant that Caterham was at a disadvantage, though this was not fully felt for some years, following considerable building development, especially at Whyteleafe and Caterham. The

SOUTHERN—Central Section

LONDON, PURLEY, WHYTELEAFE, and CATERHAM

Down — Week Days

Miles from Purley	HOUR	mrn 5	6	6	7	7	EVERY 20 mins to 10K35 mrn	E 10	E 10	Hourly to 2 44 aft	S 10	EVERY 20 mins to 2 35 aft	E 11	Hourly to 3 5 aft	E 11	Hourly to 2 25 aft
	Victoria 282 dep.	.	.	.	.	.		.	.		.		.		.	
	Charing Cross* 282 "	.	.	.	.	.		9	44		.		5		25	
	Waterloo* 282 "	.	.	.	.	.		11	46		.		7		27	
	London Bridge 282 "	16	35	55	15	35		16	51		55		11		31	
—	Purley "	46	**6**	**26**	46	59		39	**18**		**19**		38		59	
1	Kenley	49	9	29	49	**2**		42	21		23		41		**2**	
2¼	Whyteleafe	53	12	32	52	5		45	24		25		44		5	
3	Warlingham	55	14	34	54	7		47	26		27		46		7	
4¼	Caterham arr.	59	18	38	58	11		51	30		31		50		11	

Miles from Purley	HOUR	aft S 2	S 3	Hourly to 7 5 aft	3	3	Hourly to 10 44 aft	E 4	S 4	Hourly to 6 25 aft	E 4	Hourly to 6 25 aft	B 4	Hourly to 6 55 aft	And at
	Victoria 282 dep.	.	.		.	.		.	.		.		.		
	Charing Cross* 282 "	.	5		21	44		.	25		.		.		
	Waterloo* 282 "	.	7		24	46		.	27		.		.		
	London Bridge 282 "	51	11		28	51		16	31		35		55		
—	Purley "	**19**	39		59	**19**		40	59		**0**		**18**		
1	Kenley	22	42		**2**	22		43	**2**		3		21		
2¼	Whyteleafe	25	45		5	25		46	5		6		24		
3	Warlingham	27	47		7	27		48	7		8		26		
4¼	Caterham arr.	31	51		11	31		52	11		12		30		

Miles from Purley	HOUR	E 5	E 6	E 7	7	Hourly to 10 25 aft	8	Hourly to 12 5 ngt	And at	11	Sundays mrn 6	7	7	8	HALF-HOURLY to 10 2 aft	J 8	HALF-HOURLY to 11 2 aft
	Victoria 282 dep.	.	.	.	.		.			.	40	.	46	2		.	
	Charing Cross* 282 "	.	.	8	25		5			40	.	.	.	.		23	
	Waterloo* 282 "	.	.	10	27		7			.	.	.	.	.		25	
	London Bridge 282 "	18	15	14	31		11			45	.	16	.	.		30	
—	Purley "	41	38	41	58		38			**14**	**16**	59	**29**	39		58	
1	Kenley	44	41	44	**1**		41			17	19	**2**	32	42		**2**	
2¼	Whyteleafe	47	44	47	4		44			20	22	5	35	45		5	
3	Warlingham	49	46	49	6		46			22	24	7	37	47		7	
4¼	Caterham arr.	53	50	53	10		50			26	28	11	41	51		11	

Up — Week Days

Miles	HOUR	mrn 5	EVERY 20 mins to 6 53 mrn	7	EVERY 20 mins to 9 34 mn (except 9 14 mn)	And at	9	9	9	E 10	EVERY 20 mins to 4 53 aft	S 10	EVERY 20 mins to 1N54 aft	aft S 2	EVERY 20 mins to 6 33 aft
—	Caterham dep.	53		14			20	55	35	13		14		13	
1¼	Warlingham	56		18			24	59	39	17		18		17	
2¼	Whyteleafe	58		20			26	**1**	**1**	19		20		19	
3¼	Kenley	**1**		23			29	4	4	22		23		21	
4¼	Purley 282, 284 arr.	5		26			32	7	7	25		26		25	
17¾	London Bridge 284 "	31		50			55	32	32	51		50		51	
18½	Waterloo* 284 "	.		.			E59	.	36	54		.		54	
19¾	Charing Cross* 284 "	.		.			E2	.	39	57		.		58	
18	Victoria 284 "	.		.			.	.	.	.		.		.	

Miles	HOUR	And at	E 3	E 3	Hourly to 5 33 aft	E 3	Hourly to 5 52 aft	And at	E 4	E 5	E 6	E 6	6	Hourly to 10 53 aft	7	Hourly to 10 11 aft	7	Hourly to 10 32 aft
—	Caterham dep.		13	33		52			8	14	15	34	53		11		32	
1¼	Warlingham		17	37		56			12	18	18	38	57		14		35	
2¼	Whyteleafe		19	39		58			14	20	20	40	59		16		37	
3¼	Kenley		22	42		**1**			17	23	23	43	**2**		19		40	
4¼	Purley 282, 284 arr.		25	45		4			20	26	27	46	5		21		44	
17¾	London Bridge 284 "		51	**12**		30			49	50	50	**11**	31		51		**11**	
18½	Waterloo* 284 "		.	.		.			.	.	.	14	33		54		13	
19¾	Charing Cross* 284 "		.	.		.			.	.	.	17	36		57		16	
18	Victoria 284 "		.	.		.			.	.	.	.	.		.		.	

Miles	HOUR	And at	11	11	Sundays mrn 6	7	HALF-HOURLY to 10 29 aft	K 8	HALF-HOURLY to 10 8 aft	And at	aft 11	11	11
—	Caterham dep.		15	33	48	29		8			4	12	11 32
1¼	Warlingham		19	37	51	32		12			7	15	11 35
2¼	Whyteleafe		21	39	53	34		14			9	17	11 37
3¼	Kenley		24	42	56	37		17			12	20	11 40
4¼	Purley 282, 284 arr.		27	45	**0**	41		20			16	24	11 44
17¾	London Bridge 284 "		55	**15**	.	**10**		.			52	.	12 17
18½	Waterloo* 284 "		57	.	.	12		.			55	.	.
19¾	Charing Cross* 284 "		**0**	.	.	15		.			57	.	.
18	Victoria 284 "		.	.	58	.		56			.	**0**	12 16

A Kingswood and Burgh Heath
A The 9 5 mrn runs 3 mins. later on Sats and 10 15 mrn runs Sats only
B Tadworth and Walton-on-Hill
S The 1 3, 2 48, and 4 3 aft run 1 min. *earlier*
O The 11 4 mrn and 1 44 aft run 1 min. *earlier*
O The 4 44, 5 44, and 6 44 aft run Sats only
E or E Except Sats
F The 4 3 aft runs 2 mins. *earlier*
H The 5 58 aft runs 2 mins *earlier*
J The 11 53 aft runs 3 mins. *earlier* from Purley
J The 8 23 aft deps 2 mins. *earlier*
K The 6 8 aft runs 2 mins *earlier*
K The 10 15 mrn runs Sats only
L The 2 53 and 4 13 aft run 1 min. *earlier*
N The 11 14 mrn and 1 54 aft run 1 min. *earlier*
S Sats only
* Trains run between these Stations and London Bridge at frequent intervals
‡ The 11 5 aft. runs 3 mins. later from Purley

1938 time-table, when *Bradshaw* was still full of hands pointing everywhere, and an economy time-table style that was not easy to read, especially if in a hurry. This was when services were provided for those who had to work a half-day on Saturday.

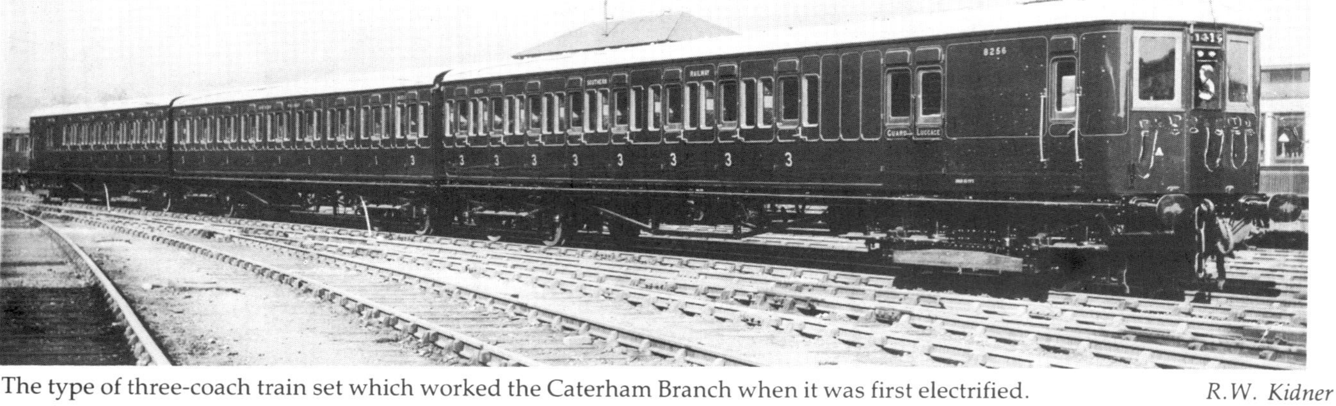

The type of three-coach train set which worked the Caterham Branch when it was first electrified. *R.W. Kidner*

three-coach set held 236–250 passengers and, incidentally, cost at that time approximately 3*d*. to run one coach one mile.[1]

The last steam passenger train to Caterham left Charing Cross at 11.37 pm on the night of Saturday, 24 March 1928, and at 7.35 am on Sunday morning there arrived the first electric train on regular service.

Until Sunday, 17 June 1928, when the full service was brought into operation, the majority of trains were adaptations of the final steam service, but the new June service provided for 54 trains up and down on week-days, and 31 up and 32 down on Sundays, with one extra to and from Purley. The electric service was better, in the aggregate, than the steam service of about 24 up and 26 down on weekdays, and 10 up and 11 down on Sundays. There was no steam train up before 7.14 am on week-days, whereas the first electric train left at 5.52 am. The up steam business service certainly provided more trains: 7.47, 8.0, 8.24, 8.38, 8.58, and 9.13, but even here the electric trains had the advantage of slightly better journey time. One praiseworthy introduction to the new electric service was the standardisation of front and rear portions of the combined trains, which now became Tattenham in front, Caterham behind. Hitherto almost anything might have happened. Sometimes the Caterham portion was in front, with the Tadworth coaches behind, or *vice versa*.

In the summer of 1930, an additional service was put into operation, on Sundays only, between Victoria and Caterham and Tattenham Corner, this providing four trains an hour to and from London.

Another innovation was the introduction of cheap single fares on both branches. 4*d*. from Caterham to Purley, and 6*d*. to East Croydon was indeed cheap – cheaper even than the bus fare.[2]

The outbreak of war in September 1939 caused a drastic curtailment of services on all lines. From 11 September the weekday service became hourly (except during the business periods which remained at three trains an hour); the Sunday service was reduced to two trains an hour (one to Charing Cross and one to Victoria). This service was maintained throughout the war, and it was not until the autumn of 1945 that an additional hourly train was put on on weekdays; from this date also, Sunday trains to and from Victoria were diverted to Charing Cross, services that had hitherto used the former route thereafter running to Coulsdon North. The full service of three trains an hour throughout the day did not return until October 1948. The 12.04 midnight train down has not been reinstated, but even before the war it was poorly patronised.

---

[1]*SR Magazine*, April 1928, p. 129.

[2]1952 single fares are: Caterham to Purley 1*s*.; to East Croydon 1*s*. 8*d*. (Since 2 March, Purley 9*d*., East Croydon 1*s*. 2*d*.) 1985 fares are: Caterham to Purley 80p; East Croydon £1 10p.

Comparatively speaking, the Caterham line suffered little damage during the war years, though the usual 'incidents' were reported from time to time and on several occasions traffic was completely stopped.

From 6 October 1941 first-class compartments on all suburban lines were converted into thirds. Even then, over-crowding during the business hours, which had become steadily worse in the 1930s, became appalling, and the three-coach service was totally inadequate. The Southern Railway could hardly be blamed (though they were) for this state of affairs: shortage of staff and rolling-stock made the position difficult, and they maintained, with some justification, that such lines as the Dartford Loop and the North Kent demanded prior consideration.[1]

After the war, complaints increased. There were other matters which irritated, too. If anything went wrong, it seemed it was always Tattenham Corner that had the through train;[2] when ice and snow lay on the rails, tired and grumbling businessmen were turned out at Purley to hang about in this coldest and draughtiest of stations to await the Caterham portion which crawled in from the siding, very often without an atom of heat in it. It became known, of course, that on those icy nights, when blue flashes lit up the sky, six coaches must run on each branch; it was necessary to provide more motor-coaches for the gradients, especially on the Tattenham line, as ice would get under the collecting shoes and cut out one or more motors.[3] What the Caterham passenger did *not* appreciate, of course, was that Tattenham should have the luxury of through trains, while he waited in the cold.

On one occasion there was very nearly a revolt. It was on one of the icy nights of the 1946–7 winter, with snow lying everywhere, and swirling before the blast through the bleak hell of Purley station. Two belated business trains had disgorged their load of Caterham passengers, and the inadequate waiting-room and dowdy bar could hold no more.[4] Some bold spirit demanded information in no uncertain

[1]These lines, of course, had a more frequent service, and the distance that had to be accomplished by a standing passenger was considerably less than between London and Caterham.

[2]Tattenham did, however, have an unpleasant experience on one occasion when on 6 August 1948, the 11.40 pm from Charing Cross had to be routed *via* Caterham! Owing to floods following heavy rain, the motorman booked to take the Caterham portion on from Purley was held up at Clock House, on the Mid-Kent line. As the motorman of the 11.40 was due to book off at Tattenham, it was decided to take the whole train on to Caterham, whence the front portion returned to Purley and on to Tattenham. In spite of all the delay, arrival there at 1.20 am was only 49 minutes late.

[3]Each three-car set had two motor-coaches. Following one of the blizzards of the 1962–3 winter, when four-coach trains were in operation, there was one occasion when a 24-coach train limped into Tattenham Corner, several hours late, having picked up broken down trains here and there on the way.

[4]The only other shelter from the blast appeared to be the Gentlemen's lavatory, which had been rendered uninhabitable on that particular night by a thick coating of ice all over the floor.

terms, and a reply was immediately forthcoming over the loud-speaker: 'The next train at Number Six platform will be for Tattenham Corner.' This was too much not only for the bold spirit, but for everyone else on the platform, and the low mumbling of protest increased in volume. Attracted by the noise, the bar customers, with nothing better to do than gaze at their beer or those curious buns and slabs of yellow Madeira cake which seem permanently to adorn refreshment rooms,[1] came tumbling out on to the platform and joined in the chorus. The occupants of the waiting-room, with nothing at all to do but gaze at each other, followed them. The deafening roar which swept Purley at that moment was followed by a further announcement over the loudspeaker: 'The next train at Number Six platform will be for the Caterham branch.' And they kept to their word.

The Caterham branch passengers were thoroughly dissatisfied with conditions, and the Councils governing the area through which the line passed received endless complaints, demands for a better service, and, of course, suggestions for improvements. It was unfortunate that so many suggestions, though given in all good faith, were from people who had no idea of the complications of railway working, and who thought it was only a question of 'more and longer trains'.

To run more trains, at any rate through the bottleneck from Purley to Windmill Bridge Junction, a short distance north of East Croydon would, at that time, have been virtually impossible, although the situation was eased when automatic colour-light signalling was introduced between East Croydon and Coulsdon North in May 1955.

Longer trains meant longer platforms at Purley and London Bridge, and nothing much could be done until this sort of alteration could be completed, and the junction with the main line made further towards London. It was not a problem that could be solved overnight.

One solution to the overcrowding trouble, suggested in the 1952 edition of this book, but frowned on, on grounds of expense as usual, would have been to provide a crossover between Reedham and Smitham – where the Chipstead Valley line runs parallel to, and on a level with, the Brighton line – to the up and down local lines serving Coulsdon North. This would have cut out Reedham and closed Coulsdon North, these trains being diverted to Tattenham Corner, and leaving Caterham with the service then in operation. This solution came in (in part) 32 years later when, on 23 January 1984, Coulsdon North was closed and some of its trains diverted to Smitham.

[1]This is not to suggest that Purley Refreshment Room was any worse than any other; in any case, it was closed, with the one on the old up main platform, many years ago.

A meeting between the Railway's Representative and the Caterham and Warlingham Council was arranged for 31 March 1949 'to air grievances'. By this time, however, the travellers' guns had been spiked somewhat by the appearance, as from 14 February, of a four-coach set on the 7.54 am up and 5.36 pm down trains, and on all trains as from 7 March. This meant that Tattenham Corner was reduced from six to four coaches. Despite greater seating capacity in the new coaches, this did reduce the overall accommodation to a certain extent.

The March meeting did, however, produce a number of reasonable grumbles, chiefly in connexion with the reduction of fares. (One shock for Caterham was to learn that fares to that station were actually slightly *below* the standard rate.) But the complaint that trains were dirty was without much justification; if so many passengers did not use the opposite seat for putting their muddy shoes on, there would have been no dirt at all. One criticism concerned the narrowness of the compartments of certain of the four-coach trains. These had been built in 1941 and were known, for some reason, as 'Queen of Sheba'. They had straight backs, narrow seats, and virtually no room for standing passengers. They were designed to hold six passengers a side, a total of 468 passengers in four coaches. The new open saloon coaches that appeared in 1946–7 were much more roomy and the standing passenger at least had comparative comfort.

The suggested re-naming of the station called 'Warlingham' (but situated nowhere near that place) caused a certain amount of stir, for the name was so obviously misleading, and passengers directed back to the previous station at Whyteleafe in order to get a bus to the village up on the hill, were justifiably angry. In the last century, this vague nomenclature did not matter much in those spacious days when people did not hurry. The opening of the Oxted line in 1884 created another station in the district, and this was called 'Upper Warlingham' ('Upper Warlingham & Whyteleafe' from 1 January 1894 to November 1901) which, though a little nearer the village, was not a particularly good name. Various new names were put forward to British Railways, the local Council suggesting Portley Wood, while the author thought the more apt, if more eccentric – as in bygone days – name of Wapses Lodge of interest. British Railways would go no further than suggesting it could be called Lower Warlingham; in actual fact, the only station that could, with any reason, be called *Lower* Warlingham was *Upper* Warlingham. So nothing was done until it was changed, without anyone really knowing much about it, to Whyteleafe South on 11 June 1956. It was one way of reminding us that, in such a dull suburban area, we could only expect dull suburban names.

1856  1956

THE CATERHAM RAILWAY CENTENARY

CELEBRATIONS ON BANK HOLIDAY MONDAY

SPECIAL STEAM TRAIN · 6th AUGUST

NON-STOP PURLEY - CATERHAM · 1878 'TERRIER' ENGINE

CIVIC RECEPTION · REGIMENTAL BAND
RAILWAY HISTORICAL EXHIBITION
MEMOIR OF CATERHAM RAILWAY

SEE SOUVENIR PROGRAMME

PRICE ONE SHILLING FROM ALL NEWSAGENTS AND BOOKSELLERS

Proceeds in aid of
CATERHAM & DISTRICT OLD PEOPLE'S WELFARE ASSOCIATION

ISSUED BY THE CATERHAM RAILWAY CENTENARY COMMITTEE · PRINTED BY ANTHONY SMITH, WESTWAY, CATERHAM

One of the posters that was displayed all over the district, before the Centenary Celebrations.

THE CATERHAM RAILWAY COMPANY

CENTENARY LUNCHEON

Soper Memorial Hall Caterham

12 for 12.30 p.m.

on Monday 6th August 1956

ADMIT ONE

PRICE TEN SHILLINGS

Centenary Luncheon Ticket.

Caterham Railway Co.
Godstone Rd.
to
CATERHA
& bac

SPECIAL
Half-Day Excursion
(G.M. 13226) 6th. AUG, 1956
Purley to
CATERHAM
and Back
see over

The trains of the Caterham Railway Company are run in connexion with those of the L.B. & S.C. and S.E. Railways, but no guarantee can be given that the trains of those Companies will run as advertised.

The two tickets issued for the special train, with a rude gesture to the main line companies printed on the back of the 'original'.

The following photographic section is of the special train for 'The Caterham Centenarian' that ran from Purley to Caterham and back on 6 August 1956:

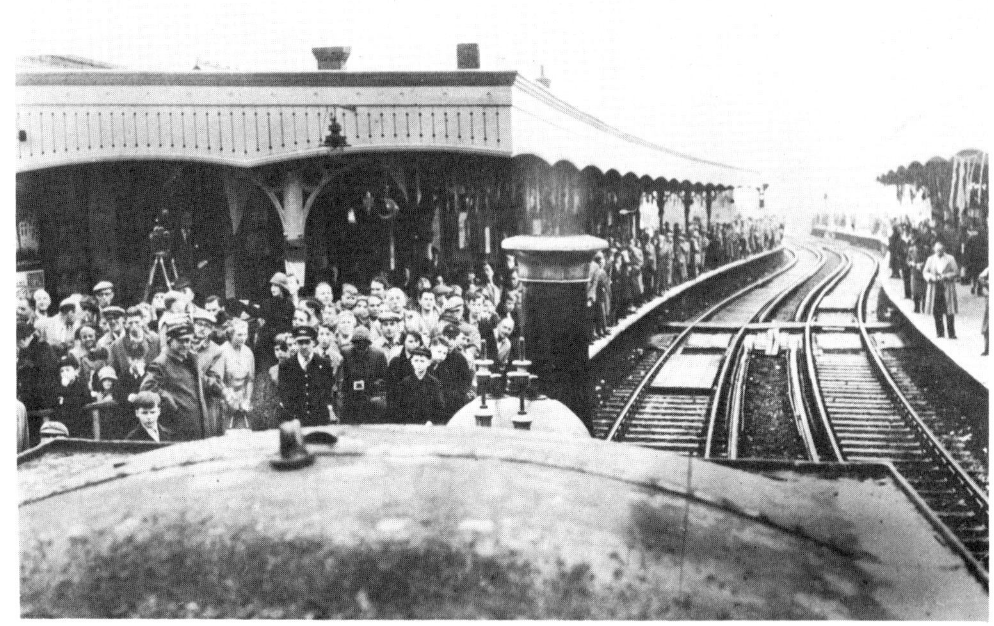

The crowds that day were very large, as can be seen from the train which was just about to leave for Caterham. *Caterham News*

'On its way' shortly after leaving Purley. *K.C. Nunn Collection*

The special near Whyteleafe South on 5 August 1956. *R.C. Riley*

A fine view of the train entering Caterham station with the 3-coach 'birdcage' set. *D.J.W. Brough*

Down train to Caterham seen here at Whyteleafe South (late Warlingham) Station on 5 August 1956. *R.C. Riley*

The 'Caterham Centenarian Special' at Caterham station on 6 August 1956. This view shows well the signal-box and signal detail. *R.C. Riley*

A view of the headboard carried by the 0–6–0 Terrier from Brighton. Caterham goods shed can be seen on the right of the photograph. *Caterham News*

The guests, including the Motive Power Superintendent and the District Traffic Superintendent of the Southern Region, are received by the Chairman and other dignitaries of the local Council (the author is to be seen, with buttonhole, standing to the right of the pillar). *Courtesy Evening News*

The Centenary, in 1956, of the opening of the line was an unexpected, if deserved, success; many people worked very hard, for a long time, to make it so. At this period, Centenary celebrations of railways were not uncommon, but they were quite often of an official nature. Initially, Caterham was a local affair. Twelve months earlier the author, who had for a long time looked forward to the event, consulted with the then local Librarian, Charles Silverthorne, on finding people who could be counted on to 'help'. This meant that the author appointed himself as Chairman of the Organizing Committee and got everyone else to do the work. There was enough enthusiasm among those interested to appoint, apart from the usual secretarial and financial officers, a 'Flowers & Shrubs' officer, responsible for decorating the station on the day, and an 'Intoxicants' officer for dealing with refreshments (there was no intention that it should be a gloomy affair). It was discovered that the proper Centenary day – August 5 for the public opening – was a Sunday and, in 1956, a *dies non* as far as jollification went. The following Monday was, in that year, an August Bank Holiday. Realizing that any running of a special train, even from Purley, would have to be worked in among 'race' specials to Tattenham Corner, made the matter immediately and automatically frowned on by any railway official. In any case, one was informed, excursions – day or half-day – had *never* been run internally on the Southern Region on August Bank Holidays.

The Divisional Superintendent of the Central Section somehow got wind of the plans being made in Caterham, and indeed the General Manager himself, and they came to the rescue in several ways, and smoothed the passage of some of the knottier problems; certain matters were overlooked and certain arrangements were made. Locomotive DS 377, once Number 35, one of Stroudley's 'Terrier' class, called *Morden*, was brought up rather secretly overnight from its shunting work at Brighton. At 7.15 am on Monday 6 August, a light engine was scheduled to leave Norwood shed for Eardley Sidings at Streatham, arriving at 7.38 to 'work the 8.02 empties to Purley'. A South Eastern & Chatham 'birdcage' three-coach set arrived at 8.43, and slipped quietly into a siding to await the next step. DS 377 then left Norwood shed at 9 am and steamed its way gently through Croydon, arriving at Purley at 9.23. The British are notorious for turning away when anything eccentric happens, and waiting passengers at East Croydon must have wondered in a self-conscious way, and even pretended not to see this diminutive engine, boiler front almost totally concealed behind a vast circular headboard proclaiming 'The Caterham Railway'. But everything was down in black and white, shipshape and Bristol fashion, and even according to railway rules, in the Special Traffic Notice. Among the miscellaneous debris of advice concerning the closing of Holland Road Halt, the milk traffic from Ffairfach (WR) to East Croydon, and the trains that were to stop out-of-course, was the announcement that the Caterham Centenarian was to leave Purley Siding as an empty train at 10.32 am and arrive at Number Six Platform at 10.35, still empty, and leave as a booked passenger train at 10.45; and, of course, it all went like clockwork. By 10.35½ the three empty coaches were loaded to bursting point; the train crew of driver, fireman, guard and inspector – all of whom had been subjected to being made up, bearded, be-wigged and dressed in mid-Victorian gear – were in position; the film and television cameras whirred. And at 10.45 to the second, this slightly comic but never-to-be-forgotten journey started.

The weather could hardly (as a hundred years previously) be said to be as brilliant. It was damp and cool, but even here luck held: violent thunderstorms were raging over the south London area, and at Tunbridge Wells, barely fifteen miles away, several inches of snow and hail were settling. Who says there are no guardian angels?

The run to Caterham could be described as uneventful, although the inspector, from his position on the footplate, had one or two moments when he kept his fingers crossed. The last mile or so of 1 in 90 brought the speed down somewhat, but locomotive *Morden*, gamely hauling its three heavily loaded coaches, just made it. And among the crowd at the London end of the Caterham platform it was reported from more than one source that a silence fell as the 'Terrier' struggled into sight through the trees round the last bend, its chimney noisily belching forth a white plume of smoke; and with the deafening cheer that followed, a great many eyes suddenly became quite moist.

From the other end of the platform a 20-strong military band was raising the station's glass roof with the rousing, welcoming sound of Nacio Herb Brown's 'Good-morning', a most appropriate number. An exhibition of railway history awaited, after the formal greetings were over; and a cocktail reception and luncheon. The reception might have been less successful if the member of the organizing committee who had volunteered to help with the bar had not inadvertently mixed dry sherry with the gin instead of dry Martini. The result was entirely satisfactory, if rather noisy, and probably put to shame the cold collation of 1856. It was undoubtedly a very successful Centenary celebration, and much of the success was due to the railway in one capacity or another. And someone must have unemotionally worked out all those little notes for the Special Traffic Notice. The bill for the special train, with all that that involved, night duties, taking water at Three Bridges, staff doing this and that, was only £36 6*s*. 8*d*.

The years that followed this unusual episode were rather flat.

In the winter of 1956–7 three extra shuttle trains were put on between Caterham and Purley in the morning rush, but a corresponding service down in the evening was not operationally possible. Two of these very useful trains lasted until the first major re-casting of services in May 1978. There was one curious extra train from Caterham to Victoria, which started in September 1964 and ran for a couple of years or so. It left Caterham at 5.24 pm and, stopping only at Whyteleafe South on the branch and at Purley, East Croydon and Clapham Junction, arrived at Victoria at 6.02. It was presumably one way of getting stock to Victoria to make up the 6.07 pm, the one Victoria to Caterham and Tattenham Corner train of the day. The odd thing about its timing was that, whereas all trains were allowed three minutes between Caterham and Whyteleafe South, this one was allowed *four*. Perhaps it was a ten-coach train and required an extra minute, so meticulous are those in authority who work out timetables. In July 1967 some reorganization of services took place, Tattenham Corner always henceforth being at the London end of a coupling-up, which meant that Caterham now took the lead on down journeys, with an allowance of one minute between arrival at Purley, uncoupling and departure of the Caterham section, with a further one minute before departure of the Tattenham section. Needless to say, this timing was never kept to.

In May 1978 the peak services were improved to four an hour, only to be reduced again to a 20-minute interval (but without the shuttles) on 23 January 1984. At the same time, Coulsdon North was closed, and some trains diverted to Smitham.

The only other event of this period that managed to make the newspapers was on 29 March 1974, when the 6.49 am mysteriously moved out of Caterham 15 minutes early, crewless and passengerless, and taking advantage of a continuous down grade, ran as far as Norwood, where it was diverted by worried railwaymen into a siding, causing some damage to set number 5323 and a buffer stop. It also seized up most of the main line, as no one knew what it might do until it could be stopped. A member of the staff emerging from the lavatory spotted it moving off and had the presence of mind to telephone the signalman that it was a runaway, thereby saving the price of a new pair of level crossing gates at Whyteleafe South.

In April 1981, colour light signalling was installed between Purley and Caterham, and was controlled locally from existing boxes, before being transferred to a temporary panel at Purley in September 1983 and then to Three Bridges on 23 January 1984. The station working at Purley was reorganized after the transfer of the signalling. The down trains in off-peak hours used the *up* platform number five, and the up trains used the old down main line platform four – a somewhat startling experience for passengers who hadn't been told. Number six platform was abandoned altogether except during peak hours. Number two platform became the down main, and number four platform became used for reversible working, as two Brighton slow trains came down that way during the hour.

It is all so very different from 1856 when the Brighton Railway re-opened 'Godstone Road', rather reluctantly, for those infernal nuisances from Caterham, refusing even to mend the holes in the rotting wooden platform, or connect the Caterham to the main line except by a back-shunt.

Since then quite a lot has been achieved, but the question people sometimes ask is: 'Has it all been for the better?'

Guard, Inspector, Fireman and Driver, dressed in period costume. The grim look on the face of the Council Chairman is probably because he had just burnt his hand patting the engine's boiler. *Courtesy Caterham News*

Caterham station in November 1985. About the only things the same as in 1952 view are the rolling stock and the manhole cover. Even the glass roof over the platform building has yet to be completed. *Brian Dagwell*

Caterham station. Exterior view November in 1985 showing the Waitrose Supermarket development. *Brian Dagwell*

Whyteleafe station, November 1985, and a number of changes: signal-box demolished, installation of colour-light signalling and new and austere footbridge with the level crossing now automatic. *Brian Dagwell*

Whyteleafe South station (late Warlingham) November 1985. *Brian Dagwell*

Kenley station in November 1985. Very little change except that the 'Gentlemen' department has disappeared. *Brian Dagwell*

Purley station in November 1985. Photographed from the same position as the 1952 photograph. *Brian Dagwell*

Appendix I

List of Principal Dates

1801	May 21	Surrey Iron Rly obtained Act of Incorporation.
1803	May 17	Croydon, Merstham & Godstone Rly obtained Act of Incorporation.
1803	July 26	Surrey Iron Rly opened from Wandsworth to Croydon.
1805	July 24	Croydon, Merstham & Godstone Rly opened to Merstham.
1836	June 21	South-Eastern Rly obtained Act of Incorporation, later abandoned for that of 14 June 1839.
1836	Dec. 14	London & Greenwich Rly opened to Deptford.
1837	July 15	London & Brighton Rly obtained Act of Incorporation.
1839	June 5	London & Croydon Rly opened to (West) Croydon.
1841	July 12	London & Brighton Rly opened to Hayward's Heath.
1841	Sept. 21	London & Brighton Rly extended to Brighton.
1842	May 26	South-Eastern Rly opened from Reigate (Redhill) to Tonbridge; and took over section from Reigate to Stoat's Nest from the Brighton Rly, at cost price.
1844	April 16	Reigate stations closed and concentrated on present site (Redhill).
1846	July 27	London & Brighton and London & Croydon Rlys amalgamated as London, Brighton & South Coast Rly.
1847	Sept. 30	Godstone Road station, LBSC, closed.
1848	July 10	Agreement between LBSC and SE Rlys not to make lines into each other's territory.
1853	Oct. 21	Correspondence opened between LBSC and SE Rlys over projected Caterham Rly.
1854	June 16	Caterham Rly receives Royal Assent to its Act.
1854	Nov. 3	Agreement between LBSC and SE Rlys not to give any assistance to any new lines in the district.
1855	Mar. 5	Ceremony of cutting the first sod of Caterham Rly near Burnt Wood.
1855	Nov. 29	Agreement between LBSC and SE Rlys concerning traffic between London and junction with the Caterham Rly.
1856	Aug. 4	Formal opening of Caterham Rly.
1856	Aug. 5	Public opening of Caterham Rly for goods and passengers. Godstone Road station reopened.

1856	Oct.–Nov.	Godstone Road station renamed Caterham Junction.
1856	Nov.	Coulsdon station renamed Kenley.
1856	Nov.	Court Case: Caterham Rly *v.* LBSC and SE Rlys.
1857	Mar.	Caterham Rly offer to sell to LBSC for £23,700.
1858	July 22	Court Case: Caterham Rly *v.* Furness, contractor.
1858	Nov.	Caterham Rly apply to Parliament for powers to sell or lease to SE Rly.
1859	Apr./May	Caterham train service reduced to two trains daily.
1859	July 21	Caterham Rly transferred to SE Rly.
1861	Feb.	First slip-coach service introduced at Caterham Junction.
1862	Feb.	Sunday service to Caterham discontinued.
1862	Oct.	Scandal at Caterham Junction. Great publicity given to LBSC-SE feud.
1863	Jan.	Workmen's tickets introduced from Caterham and Warlingham to London.
1864	Mar. 2	Agreement between LBSC and SE Rlys similar to that of 1848 (q.v.).
1865	May	Sunday service to Caterham reinstated.
1866	April 30	Collision near Caterham Junction. Four killed.
1867	April	Late night train to Caterham put into service on Thursdays.
1869–70		LBSC and SE Rlys pool Caterham Junction receipts. Fares raised.
1873	Sept. 22	Passenger fatally injured crossing the line at Caterham Junction. Board of Trade demand improvements there.
1874	Oct.	New subway and other alterations at Caterham Junction.
1873–82		Bills deposited by several local railway companies, all of which were abortive.
1884	Mar. 10	Croydon, Oxted & East Grinstead Rly opened. Jointly worked by LBSC and SE Rlys.
1888	Oct. 1	Caterham Junction renamed Purley.
1893		Chipstead Valley Rly incorporated.
1897	Nov. 2	Chipstead Valley Rly opened to Kingswood.
1897–1900		General improvements, including doubling of line between Purley and Caterham.
1898		Purley Loco. Shed opened.
1899	Nov. 5	LBSC extend local line from South Croydon to Stoat's Nest.
1899		Purley station rebuilt.
1900	Jan. 1	New Caterham station opened. Whyteleafe station opened. Train service improved.

1900	Aug. 6	Act obtained by SE&LCD Rlys to construct line from near Sanderstead to Caterham and Chipstead Valley lines.
1900	July 1	Kingswood to Tadworth opened.
1900	July 2	Line doubled between Purley and Tadworth.
1901	June 4	Tadworth to Tattenham Corner opened.
1917	Jan. 1	Train services cut during emergency. Fares raised 50 per cent.
1923	Jan 1	Formation of Southern Railway.
1923	Sept.	Second-class fares abolished on SE section.
1928	Mar. 25	Inauguration of electric service between London and Caterham and Tattenham Corner.
1939	Sept. 11	Reduction in train services due to the war.
1941	Oct. 6	First-class abolished on suburban trains.
1949	Feb. 14	New four-coach set appears on Caterham and Tattenham branches (7.54 up and 5.36 down).
1949	Mar. 7	New four-coach sets on all Caterham and Tattenham trains.
1955	May 7–8	Colour light signalling, E. Croydon to Coulsdon.
1956	Aug. 6	Caterham Railway Centenary held.
1974	Mar. 29	Runaway train from Caterham diverted at Norwood and crashes.
1978	May	Peak services improved to four an hour.
1981	April	Colour light signalling installed on branch, operated from local boxes.
1983	Sept.	Signalling transferred to Purley. Purley station platform working reorganized.
1984	Jan. 23	Signalling transferred to Three Bridges. Coulsdon North closed and service transferred to Smitham.

Enemy action at Purley, in the fork between the Chipstead Valley and the main lines. An incident which occurred on the evening of 18 August 1940. Purley South signal-box is on the right.

The result of the collision between up and down trains outside Caterham station in June 1945. Both drivers were killed, and several passengers injured.

Appendix II

Accidents

It is generally agreed that accidents will always happen, despite all the rules and regulations that are made. In this respect, however, the South-Eastern and London, Chatham & Dover Companies had a remarkable freedom from accidents, and this record was continued after grouping by the Southern Railway. The Brighton, who served a considerable area covered by this book, also had a good record of immunity. For those interested, a list of the more serious accidents in the district is shown below.

1866 April 30 — CATERHAM JUNCTION. The 8.0 pm from Brighton to London Bridge collided with a train of chalk wagons a short distance north of the station, owing to a signalman's error. The engine went over the embankment, and several of the 15 carriages were smashed. Two passengers and two servants were killed, and a number of passengers injured.

1894 Dec. 22 — PURLEY. Collision between SE engine and Caterham portion of the 6.05 pm down from Charing Cross, causing injuries to six passengers. The Brighton admitted sole liability for the accident (which may have been due to a signalling error).

1929 Dec. 16 — PURLEY. The 4.44 pm from Tattenham Corner collided, through an error of judgment, with the 4.53 pm from Caterham, already standing in the platform, both trains normally joining up here. There was dense fog at the time, visibility being less than 10 yards. One coach was partly telescoped, and six others damaged. Owing to fouling of the down line, single line working was put into operation between Purley and Kenley, and Tattenham passengers were diverted to Coulsdon North, a shuttle service running between Smitham and Tattenham. One passenger was seriously injured, and three others slightly injured.

1934 April 1 — CATERHAM. The 10.23 pm from Charing Cross collided head-on with the 11.8 pm from Caterham to Purley outside Caterham station. Caterham consists of two platform lines with a single island platform between them. The 11.08 train was erroneously signalled out, when the 10.23 had been signalled as crossing its path. Although damage was done to both trains, there were no cases of serious injury.

1945	June 26	CATERHAM. The 8.55 am from London Bridge collided head-on with the 9.34 am from Caterham to Charing Cross at the same spot as in the 1934 accident. The 8.55 was running late, and, as the 9.34 would be able to make up time to Purley, the down train was signalled in first. The motorman of the up train, on being signalled by the guard, left without observing the starting signal against him, with the resultant collision. Overturning of the motor coach of the up train caused a heavy short circuit and fire broke out. Both drivers were killed, and one passenger seriously injured.
1947	Mar. 14	LONDON BRIDGE. The 8.04 am Tattenham Corner and 8.14 am from Caterham, which were joined at Purley, collided with the buffer stops at No. 10 platform. Fifteen passengers injured.
1947	Oct. 24	SOUTH CROYDON. The 8.04 am from Tattenham Corner and 8.14 am from Caterham, which were joined at Purley, collided, in fog, with the 7.33 am from Hayward's Heath and Reigate a short distance south of South Croydon Junction Box. The Tattenham train had been improperly allowed to approach and pass through Purley Oaks under clear signals. The Hayward's Heath train was estimated to have been carrying about 800 passengers and the Tattenham and Caterham train about 1,000. 32 passengers and the driver were killed, and nearly 60 more or less seriously injured.
1960	Feb. 22	8.15 am from Caterham collided heavily with 8.04 am from Tattenham Corner, standing in Purley station. Eight injured.
1974	Mar. 29	Runaway train from Caterham to Norwood. No injuries. *See page* 102.

Appendix III

Fare Increases

The single fares shown apply between London Bridge and Caterham. There was, normally, a proportionally cheaper rate from the intermediate stations.

From			1st		2nd		3rd		Gov.	
			s.	*d.*	*s.*	*d.*	*s.*	*d.*	*s.*	*d.*
August		1856	3	4	2.	10	2	1	1	6
May		1857	3	0	2	6	2	0	1	6
		1861	3	0	2	3	1	3	1	3
		1865**A**	2	8	2	0	1	3	1	3
		1870	3	2	2	6	1	3	1	3
		1900	3	2	2	3	1	3	1	3
		1914	2	11	2	0	1	3	–	
Jan.	1	1917	4	4½	3	0	1	10½	–	
Aug.	6	1920	5	1½	3	6	2	2½	–	
Jan.	1	1923	3	2	**B**		1	11	–	
Jan.		1928**C**	3	4	–		2	0	–	
Oct.	1	1937**D**	3	4	–		2	0	–	
May	1	1940	3	10	–		2	4	–	
Dec.		1940	4	0	–		2	5	–	
July	1	1946	–		–		2	9	–	
Oct.	1	1947	–		–		3	3	–	
Mar.	2	1952	–		–		2	8	–	
		1985	–		£2.20		–		–	

Notes

A–LBSC fares to Caterham Junction were: 1st, 2*s.* 3*d.*; 2nd, 1*s.* 9*d.*; 3rd, 1*s.* 1*d.* – whereas the SE charged the same fares as to Caterham.
B–2nd class fares abolished on SE&C section at end of September 1923.
C–Southern Rly levelled up a number of fares that were below standard rate.
D–5 per cent. increase (see below) did not affect Caterham branch, but was included in May 1940 figure.

Authorised increases and decreases

From Jan.	1	1917	50 per cent. increase.
From Aug.	6	1920	Further 25 per cent. increase.
From Jan.	1	1923	25 per cent. decrease. Basic rate of 1½*d.* per mile standard (3rd class).
From Oct.	1	1937	5 per cent. increase.
From May	1	1940	10 per cent. increase.
From Dec.		1940	6 per cent. increase.
From July	1	1946	16⅔ per cent. increase.
From Oct.	1	1947	16½ per cent. increase.
From Mar.	2	1952	28.4 per cent. decrease.

Appendix IV

Locomotives in use on the Caterham Branch

(For early history see page 37)

The only locomotive known to have been stationed in the small shed at Caterham was a Stirling 'Q' Class 0–4–4T No. 235, built in 1887. She went to Purley on the opening of the shed there in 1898, and was later transferred to Orpington. That and a sister engine, No. 367, built in 1891, did most of the Caterham branch work. No. 367 was stationed at Redhill until Purley shed was opened.

In the early 1900s Purley shed was the last home of a number of veteran engines. Several of the Cudworth 2–4–0s finished their days on the Caterham and Tadworth branches, including Nos. 4, 34, 61, 63, 71, 75, 92, 221, 223 and 229. Some of these were on the duplicate list and carried an 'A' suffix to their numbers. In 1902 some of the 2–4–0 'Ironclads' of the 271–8 batch went to Purley, some for use on the Caterham branch. There had been twenty of this type, ordered by A.M. Watkin (son of the SER Chairman), designed by John Ramsbottom, formerly of Crewe, and built by contractors in 1876. Several ex-LC&DR locomotives were there at this time, including three Martley 0–6–0s, four 2–4–0s, and one 'M' Class 4–4–0.

Between 1910 and 1914 Kirtley 'M1' Class 4–4–0s 635, 636 and 'M.2' 638 spent their last days working from Purley shed, Stirling 'O' Class 0–6–0s 131, 286 and 334 being there also. By this time, however, large numbers of Wainwright 'H' Class 0–4–4Ts were in service, and up to the time of electrification they gradually replaced the old Stirling 0–4–4Ts which had predominated on the branches since the 'eighties. At the end of 1919, the Purley allocation included 'H' Class 16, 162, 164, 177, 295 and 540, 'Q' Class 346, 414 and 424, and 'Q.1' Class 363 and 413.

The daily goods train provided the only regular steam working over the Caterham branch in 1952, the engine usually being an ex-LB&SCR 'C.2x' Class 0–6–0 from Bricklayers Arms Depot. This working was carried out from New Cross Gate until the closure of that depot in 1948. During 1950 the Diesel Mechanical locomotive No. 11001 appeared several times on this duty. There were occasional special trains, usually run at night, carrying armoured vehicles to or from Caterham, in connexion with the Guards' Barracks there.

Kenley lost its goods service 3 April 1961; Whyteleafe and Caterham 28 September 1964.

German built 'L' Class locomotive 4–4–0 No. 777 on the turntable at Caterham prior to working the 6.30 pm (SO) to Charing Cross. These were primarily main line engines and it may have been on a 'running in' turn or working a 'filling in' turn. *Late Hemming Collection*

'Q' Class 0–4–4T No. 424 at Caterham in 1913 with driver J. Challeigne, fireman S. Dulake and guard Morley. No. 424 was withdrawn in 1927. *Late Hemming Collection*

'F1' Class 4–4–0 No. 156 at Caterham with driver H. Carter. Built in 1893 and fitted with a domed boiler in 1906, it was used for Royal Train duties from 1908 to 1913, hence its copper capped chimney and highly polished finish. It was not withdrawn until 1947 having had a spell on loan to the LMS at Bristol during the war. Note the station-master's house in the distance.

Late Hemming Collection

Stirling 'O.1' Class 0–6–0 No. 389 at Caterham on the 1.45 pm freight to Bricklayers Arms. Built in 1893 and reboilered in 1906, it survived until 1949. It may be just ex works as it looks remarkably clean for a goods engine.

Late Hemming Collection

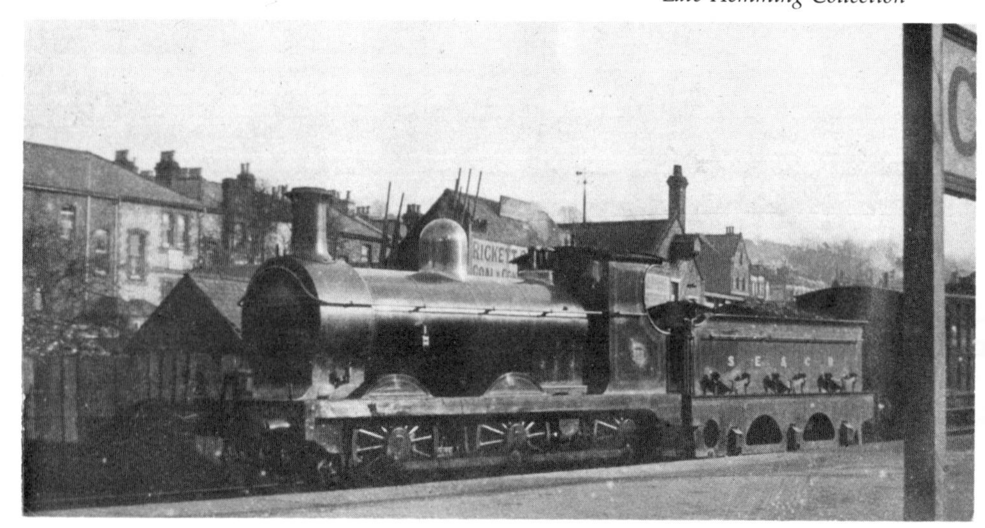

Appendix V

Rolling-stock in use on the Caterham and Chipstead Valley Branches

1. **1923 to March 1928.** Despite the fact that both branches were, officially, transferred to the Central (Brighton) Section, operationally they remained in the Eastern section, and stock used was ex-SE&C.
2. **March 1928 to March 1949.** Until about the middle 1930s SE&C rolling-stock, converted to electric, was predominant. Much of it consisted of South-Eastern four- and six-wheelers, two of which, on new underframes, made the normal eight-wheel coach. Latterly, a number of ex-LB&SC Rly coaches made their appearance, and, now and again, ex-L&SW stock.

   Seating capacity of a three-car train was officially 236 in March 1928,[1] but of recent years was described as 250.[2]
3. **From March 1949.** Four-coach sets, which can be divided as follows:[3]

   (*a*) 4101 type: Built 1941. 10 sets constructed (4101–4110). Exceptionally narrow compartments. Seat six a side. Total seating capacity, 468.

   (*b*) 4111 type: Built 1946. 10 sets constructed (4111–4120); (additional 23 sets numbers 4355–4376 constructed 1947–8 of similar type). All-compartment coaches. Seat six a side. Total seating capacity, 420.

   (*c*) 4121 type: Built 1946–7. 10 sets constructed (4121–4130). Composed of one all-compartment coach and three semi-open saloon coaches. Seat six a side in compartment coaches, and five a side in saloon. Total seating capacity, 382.

   (*d*) 4277 type: Standard full saloon type. Built 1948–9. 34 sets constructed (4277–4299 and 4378–4387[4]). Composed of one all-compartment coach and three open saloon type. Similar seating arrangements as 4121 type. Seats 386.

   (*e*) 4621 type: Built 1949–51. As 4277 type. 134 sets constructed (4621–4754). Seating capacity, 386.

   (*f*) 5001 type: Has continued to be constructed ever since. There is a possibility that the 455 stock, now in use on the Southern's Western Section, with automatic opening doors, could one day be in use in this area. It is simply, in my opinion, a glorified London Transport tube train.

---

[1] *SR Magazine*, April 1928, p. 129.

[2] Ministry of Transport Report on South Croydon accident, October 1947.

[3] A number of these have been constructed with new framework on old underframes.

[4] Number 4377 appears to have been an experiment in open-saloon type. It consists of three compartment coaches and one open saloon.

Appendix VI

Headcodes in use between London and Caterham and Tattenham Corner

	Letters Old Stock	Numbers New Stock
Charing Cross *or* Cannon Street to Tattenham Corner[1]	S̈	01
Charing Cross *or* Cannon Street to Caterham[2]	S	93
Tattenham Corner *or* Caterham to Charing Cross	S̈	01
Tattenham Corner *or* Caterham to Cannon Street	Ṡ	93
London Bridge to Tattenham Corner[1]	T̈	85
London Bridge to Caterham[2]	Ḧ	81
Victoria to Tattenham Corner[1] (not in regular use)	Ī	38
Victoria to Caterham[2] (not in regular use)	L̄	80
Purley to Caterham *or* Caterham to Purley	P	3
Purley to Tattenham Corner *or* Tattenham Corner to Purley	Ṗ	2

The Letters and Numbers have been left for historical interest. The present headcode between Caterham and London Bridge or Charing Cross and *vice versa* is 93. Normally the Tattenham Corner section is at the London end of a coupled-up train in which case the headcode is 97. Purley to Caterham or *vice versa* is 43; Purley to Tattenham Corner or *vice versa* is 47.

[1]With or without Caterham portion in rear.
[2]With or without Tattenham Corner portion in rear.

Appendix VII

Official table of distances on the Branch

	Miles	Ch.
Purley	0	0
Purley East Junction	0	10
Kenley	1	8
Whyteleafe	2	39
Warlingham (Whyteleafe South)	3	0
Caterham	4	50

Index

* *Denotes that the reference is to be found in a footnote.*

KEY TO FOLD OUT MAP

For those readers who like tracing place-names on maps the following lesser-known names can be found on the reproduction of the Ordnance Survey map fold out:

Burntwood Bridge E6
Godstone Quarries E/F10
Half Moon Inn (site of) E7
Halliloo Farm F6
Harestone Valley D9
Hayes Lane Bridge C3
Kenley House C5
Manor Cottage (Caterham Manor) E6
Marden Park G9
Money Pit Terminus C7
Mount Pleasant E8
Portley D7
Riddles Down C3
Rose & Crown D4
Stoat's Nest Old station A3
Tillingdown E8
Tupwood E10
Tyler's Green E11
Wapses Lodge E6
Warlingham Village F5
Willey Heath Terminus C9

Footnote to Folding Map opposite:

The Surrey & Sussex Junction Railway (plans deposited Nov. 1864) followed the course of the Croydon & Oxted line.

Plans for the Redhill, Bletchingley & Godstone Light Railway were deposited Nov. 1869: the scheme was not proceeded with.

There was, in addition, a plan for a line from Upper Warlingham station to Upper Caterham (1888). The SER did not approve, and plans were not deposited.